BY DONALD HONIG

NONFICTION

Baseball When the Grass Was Real
Baseball Between the Lines
The Man in the Dugout
The October Heroes
The Image of Their Greatness (with Lawrence Ritter)
The 100 Greatest Baseball Players of All Time (with Lawrence Ritter)
The Brooklyn Dodgers: An Illustrated Tribute
The New York Yankees: An Illustrated History
Baseball's 10 Greatest Teams
The Los Angeles Dodgers: The First Quarter Century
The National League: An Illustrated History
The American League: An Illustrated History
The Boston Red Sox: An Illustrated Tribute
Baseball America
The New York Mets: The First Quarter Century
The World Series: An Illustrated History
Baseball in the '50s
The All-Star Game: An Illustrated History
Mays, Mantle, Snider: A Celebration
The Greatest Pitchers of All Time
The Greatest First Basemen of All Time
Baseball in the '30s
The Donald Honig Reader
Baseball: The Illustrated History of America's Game
1959: The Year That Was
American League MVPs
National League Rookies of the Year
National League MVPs
American League Rookies of the Year
1961: The Year That Was
The Power Hitters
The Boston Red Sox: An Illustrated History
The Greatest Catchers of All Time
The St. Louis Cardinals: An Illustrated History
The Chicago Cubs: An Illustrated History
The Greatest Shortstops of All Time
The Cincinnati Reds: An Illustrated History

FICTION

Sidewalk Caesar
Walk Like a Man
The Americans
Divide the Night
No Song to Sing
Judgment Night
The Love Thief
The Severith Style
Illusions
I Should Have Sold Petunias
The Last Great Season
Marching Home

THE PHILADELPHIA PHILLIES

AN ILLUSTRATED HISTORY

DONALD HONIG

Simon & Schuster
New York   London   Toronto   Sydney   Tokyo   Singapore

Simon & Schuster
Simon & Schuster Building
Rockefeller Center
1230 Avenue of the Americas
New York, NY 10020

Copyright © 1992 by Donald Honig

Designed by Robert Bull Design
Manufactured in the United States of America

1   3   5   7   9   10   8   6   4   2

Library of Congress Cataloging-in-Publication Data

Honig, Donald.
  Philadelphia Phillies / by Donald Honig.
     p.   cm.
  Includes index.
  1. Philadelphia   Phillies   (Baseball   team—History.
  I. Title.
GV875.P45H66   1992
796.357´64´0974811—dc20   91-38774
                                                   CIP

ISBN 0-671-76107-2

For my nephew, George Honig

ACKNOWLEDGMENTS

I am deeply indebted to a number of people for their generous assistance in photo research and help in gathering the photographs reproduced in this book. Special thanks go to Michael P. Aronstein and Chuck Singer of TV Sports Mailbag; to Patricia Kelly and her colleagues at the National Baseball Hall of Fame and Museum at Cooperstown, New York; and to Steve Gietschier, chief archivist of *The Sporting News.*

Also, for their advice and counsel, a word of thanks to the following: Stanley Honig; David Markson; Lawrence Ritter; Douglas Mulcahy; Mary E. Gallagher; Louis Kiefer, Jeffrey Neuman; "Baltimore Jim" Marino; Phil Murphy; and Tom, Mike, and Jim Brookman.

And a special note of thanks to my editor Paul Aron.

CONTENTS

	Introduction	11
ONE	A Brand-New Game	13
TWO	Back in Business	15
THREE	Toward the Modern Era	21
FOUR	New Century, New League	31
FIVE	Alexander the Great	45
SIX	Pennant	53
SEVEN	Bombs Away	65
EIGHT	More Tough Going	85
NINE	The War Years	109
TEN	Rousing from Hibernation	125
ELEVEN	After Thirty-Five Years	137
TWELVE	Enter Gene Mauch	167
THIRTEEN	The Road to Glory	187
FOURTEEN	Victories and Disappointments	201
FIFTEEN	The Big One	215
APPENDIX	Phillies League Leaders	249
	Index	251

First the ball club joins the city, building a home there and adopting the city's name. And then the ball club puts the city's name on its uniforms and claims to be representative. Shortly, people will second the nomination by coming to the ballpark and spending money and sitting in the fresh air and cheering for the team. It has never taken long for the fusing between fan and team to occur, and once achieved, an almost unbreakable bond has been established. A sort of emotional infection has taken place, a benign virus laid in the blood, with its own genetic code and heritable factors. How else to explain being told, "We've been Phillies fans in our family for more than one hundred years"?

There was better reason to be Athletics fans, for before migrating to Kansas City in 1954, that Philadelphia club had won six pennants before the Phillies took their first and nine while the Phillies still had just the one.

But the Phillies had got there first (not that this necessarily implies preferences; the Braves were in Boston before the Red Sox and were forced to depart when the century was at midpoint), joining—rejoining, actually—the National League in 1883 and remaining through times thick and thin, and no ball club has ever had it thinner (see the period from the 1920s through the mid-1940s). The crowds diminished accordingly—pitcher Kirby Higbe said that "it got to a point where they were afraid to boo us because we outnum-

bered them." But that was the reflection of an inept ball club, not forgone loyalties, for when the club improved the crowds swelled. Nobody ever told the Phillies to get out of town, as they had suggested even the revered Connie Mack do when his teams fell on extended hard times. The Phillies, for better or worse, had joined the city.

This was the team that gave baseball its first "greatest outfield of all time" in the 1890s with Sliding Billy Hamilton, Sam Thompson, and Ed Delahanty. As the new century gradually matured, this was the team that flashed the record-book talents of Grover Cleveland Alexander, a pitcher seldom equaled and never bettered. At exactly the midcentury point, the team became known as "The Whiz Kids," led to a pennant by the tireless pitching machine known as Robin Roberts. In 1980 the Phillies survived the most thrilling pennant playoff series in history and went on to win the team's first world championship, led by the slugging of Mike Schmidt and the pitching of Steve Carlton. And although Phillie pennants had seemed to come with the frequency of Halley's comet, they won another banner just three years later, leading one of their longtime fans to say, "Well, they've proved that you don't have to wait a lifetime between pennants."

And so the Phillies go into the future, the realm of the optimist, secure in baseball's creed that with some timely hitting, good pitching, and a couple of breaks . . .

A BRAND-NEW GAME

The United States was less than one hundred years old when it began to embrace baseball. In the years before the Civil War, Philadelphians, among others, were discovering the joys of watching young men hitting a ball and running around the bases, those baseball basics that remain unchanged to this day. It was all there from the very beginning—hits, runs, errors—subject to polish and refinement, true, but a century and a half later it would still be recognizable to its progenitors, its growth and development strictly organic.

In the beginning it was a game played primarily by young men of the middle and upper classes, amateurs playing for the sheer fun of it. Philadelphia had a number of teams, including the Olympics, Winonas, Uniteds, Benedicts, and one whose name still answers to the roll call—the Athletics.

During and after the Civil War the spread of baseball was rapid and extensive, the game's erupting popularity attracting more and more young men to the playing fields. Inevitably, with more players, the game improved, become more competitive, with greater emphasis placed upon winning.

In 1863 the game of amateurs began turning serious when the Athletics hired for pay Alfred J. Reach, second baseman of the Brooklyn Eckfords. Reach was paid around $25 a week for his services, making him one of the first, if not the first, professional baseball player. (A few years later Reach started the sporting goods company that bore his name, which for years was stamped on American League baseballs.)

In 1871 the National Association, baseball's first professional league, was formed. This circuit, which was to prove to be a shakedown cruise for the National League, consisted of nine teams, including the Philadelphia Athletics, who set up operation at a field at Twenty-fifth and Jefferson Streets, which at the time resembled a city suburb.

The National Association was truly a modest beginning, with clubs averaging around thirty games each. The winners of that first championship, all those sunny American summers ago, were the Philadelphia Athletics, with a record of 22–7. The star of the team was Adrian ("Cap") Anson, who joined the club in 1872 and remained until 1875. Anson later joined the Chicago entry in the National League and went on to become the nineteenth century's most acclaimed player.

A second Philadelphia team, nicknamed Quakers, joined the National Association in 1873 and a third in 1875, when the ramshackle league began to teeter.

Bedeviled by rowdyism in the stands, drunken players on the field, gambling, thrown games, and franchises that came and went like so many itinerants, the National Association was foredoomed. But William Hulbert had seen the better side of things—a populace that was enchanted by the game and willing to pay money to watch it. What organized baseball needed, Hulbert reasoned, was strong central leadership and even stronger supervision.

A Chicago businessman who owned that city's franchise in the National Association, Hulbert resolved to save the fledgling game from extinction. Accordingly, in a move that proved to be momentous in the history of American sports, he decided to allow the existing league to crumble and start a new structure—the National League.

On February 2, 1876, the year of the nation's Centennial, Hulbert gathered with a group of like-minded men in a room in New York's Grand Central Hotel and laid before them his proposition: a new league, run under strict business principles,

William Hulbert saw a future for baseball in America.

with a charter of rules carefully written and rigidly enforced. Foremost among the new strictures was the banning of alcohol sales at a ballpark, a crackdown on rowdyism and profanity, the immediate disbarment of any player found betting on games, and an obligation on the part of every team to complete their schedules. Also, to ensure franchise stability, Hulbert insisted that every member city be of no less than 75,000 in population.

With a schedule of approximately seventy games, the charter members of the new league were Philadelphia, New York, Boston, Chicago, St. Louis, Hartford, Louisville, and Cincinnati. The Philadelphia club chosen was the Athletics, with several players enrolled from the disbanded Quakers.

National League baseball came to Philadelphia on April 22, 1876, with the Athletics losing to Boston 6–5, in a game played before some 3,000 customers on the grounds at Twenty-fifth and Jefferson. It was an inauspicious beginning to what would prove to be a dismal season that ended with the club's summary expulsion from the league.

After stumbling through a summer in which they had won only 14 of their 59 games and enduring a thinning of their financial resources, the Athletics decided not to make a final western trip. The New York Mutuals, also freighted with a dreary season, did the same. The feeling among the ownerships of these clubs was that because they represented the league's largest cities they could flout the rules. But William Hulbert and his colleagues would have none of it. The league booted the clubs out of the league.

Major-league baseball returned to Philadelphia in 1882 when the city placed a franchise in the newly formed American Association, put together to compete with the National League. This club remained in the rival league until the American Association collapsed in 1891. Philadelphia also had representation in two one-year upstart major leagues, the Union Association (1884) and the Players' League (1890), a concoction formed by players who were dissatisfied with what they felt was the owners' high-handed treatment of them.

It wasn't until 1883 that the Phillies returned to their ancestral nestings in the National League, and there they have remained to this day.

Concerned about competition from the American Association, the National League decided in 1883 to return New York and Philadelphia to its rolls. Colonel A. G. Mills, who had succeeded the recently deceased William Hulbert as league president, moved the Troy, New York, franchise downstate to New York and then the Worcester, Massachusetts, club to Philadelphia. The man Mills induced to back the Philadelphia team was Alfred Reach, the pioneer professional ball player, who was now a successful sporting goods manufacturer, with a large retail store on Market Street and an ever-expanding factory in Kensington. Reach was in business partnership with another man whose name was destined for long-lasting connotations in baseball—Benjamin Shibe, onetime manufacturer of whips and a connoisseur of leather, who was joined with Reach in turning out baseballs and gloves.

The club leased a parcel of land in the city's northeastern section that was bound by Twenty-fourth Street, Columbia Avenue, Twenty-fifth Street, and Ridge Avenue. A brigade of carpenters hammered together a modest wooden grandstand and bleachers, working against a rapidly approaching deadline—May 1, 1883, opening day. Christened Recreation Park, the place was ready on time to accommodate the team that by general agreement was to be known as the "Phillies."

"It tells you who we are and where we're from," said Reach.

After the team's first season, however, a lot of locals probably wished the Phillies were somebody else from elsewhere, as the team spent the summer of 1883 compiling a record of 17 victories and 81 losses. In that era of two-man pitching staffs, the club sent a gentleman named John Coleman out to a slow-torture season of 12 wins and 48 losses.

Of the players on that first Phillies outfit, history has deigned to take note of first baseman Sid Farrar, and that only because his daughter Geraldine was to become one of the silver-voiced sopranos of the Metropolitan Opera during the first two decades of the twentieth century.

That first clunking finish was ominous, because although they were not to have another basement wrap up until 1904, the Phillies have suffered, through the 1990 season, a National League record 24 last-place finishes.

Reach, however, was not discouraged. Because things obviously could not get any worse, they had, logically, to get better.

"We spent a year finding ourselves," he said, and went on to insist that they would learn from their mistakes, which we are told is always the first paving block on the road to success.

The determined Reach went out and hired to run the team the man he claimed was the game's greatest manager, Harry Wright.

Harry Wright certainly had the credentials. English-born (as was Reach), Harry, a former cricket player, had in 1869 and 1870 managed the Cincinnati Reds, the country's first openly proclaimed professional baseball team, starring his younger brother George, the game's first superstar. The lavishly bewhiskered Harry went on to manage four Boston pennant winners in the National Association, then spent six years running that city's National League entry, taking pennants in 1877 and 1878, and in 1882–1883 managed Providence, also in the National League. Now he was taking over the Phillies, a job he would hold for ten years.

The Phillies' first star player was Charlie Ferguson, a multitalented young man who joined the club in 1884. Primarily a pitcher that year (he

Baseball pioneer Harry Wright, who managed the Phillies from 1884 through 1893.

was 21–25), he also played outfield and second base. One contemporary said of Ferguson, "He was a player without a flaw or weakness, as he could do everything well. He could hit, pitch, run or field, and it made no difference where they played him."

Charlie's best year on the mound was 1886, when he was 30–9, and a year later he batted .337, dividing his time between the mound and second base. He was by now Philadelphia's prince of baseball. But in the spring of 1888 he contacted typhoid

fever and after a brief illness died on April 29, twelve days after his twenty-fifth birthday.

Another early Phillies favorite was also doomed to a short life. This was outfielder Jim Fogarty, one of the first San Franciscans to play big-league ball. Although not in Ferguson's class as a talent, Jim was one of those players whose style of play appealed to the fans. He was with the Phillies from 1884 to 1889, when he jumped to the Players'

Charlie Ferguson (1884–1887), the popular Phillies star who died in 1888 at the age of twenty-five.

never batted better than .217; third baseman Joe Mulvey, who held the job for six years and lit no fires with his bat; infielder-outfielder Ed Andrews, whose .325 average in 1887 was the best by a Phillies regular up to that time; and the man who enjoyed one of baseball's most unorthodox careers, Jack Clements, a Philadelphia native who played for the hometown club from 1884 to 1897—as a left-handed catcher. There were occasional southpaw catchers in baseball's early

Jim Fogarty (1884–1889) posing in a photographer's studio. The ball is suspended from a string.

League. When that league collapsed, he was set to return to the Phillies (who were eager to welcome him back) when he was stricken with tuberculosis—in those years an almost certain death notice—and died on May 20, 1891, just twenty-seven years old.

Other Phillies regulars of the day were infielder Charlie Bastian, who played for four years and

Third baseman Joe Mulvey (1883–1889, 1892).

Ed Andrews (1884–1889) showing how it was done in the days before players wore gloves.

days, but none with the longevity of Clements, who played for other clubs until 1900.

Another 1880s figure in Philadelphia baseball was shortstop Arthur Irwin, signed by the Phillies when the Providence club folded. Never much of a hitter, Irwin was known as an aggressive and sharp-minded player; he is also recorded as having been the first infielder to wear a glove. According to the splendid history of the Phillies by Fred Lieb and Stan Baumgartner, Irwin designed and then patented his glove and sold the patent to the Reach-Shibe firm, which began manufacturing baseball gloves.

By 1887 the Phillies were successful enough to

make Recreation Park obsolete, and Reach decided to build a new park "worthy of our team." The site selected was a debris-ridden lot bordered by Broad Street, Lehigh Avenue, Fifteenth, and Huntington. Here Reach erected what for the time was quite a baseball palace. Where all previous parks had been wooden in structure and thus vulnerable to fire, Reach raised a structure of steel and brick that was one of the game's early wonders. With a seating capacity of more than 12,000, it was more than large enough to accommodate the baseball-hungry locals. A pavilion holding the better seats was topped by a pair of 75-foot-high turrets, while a 165-foot-high turret stood over the main entrance. Underneath the stands were the forerunners of today's parking facilities—sheds for more than fifty carriages. Officially designated "The Philadelphia Baseball Park," it was informally referred to as the "Huntington Park" or the "Huntington Street Grounds."

The new park opened on April 30, 1887, with 20,000 people, including standees packed behind outfield ropes, shoehorned into the place. It was surely Philadelphia's event of the year, with the Phillies and the opposing New York Giants paraded in open carriages up Broad Street to the park. After the appropriate music and speeches, the Phillies baptized their new home with a rapid-fire attack: The first nine men to go to bat in the bottom of the first inning rapped hits, sending the club off to a 19–10 victory.

The Phillies finished second in 1887, 3½ games behind Detroit (in those pre–American League years a National League outpost). The club ran three effective pitchers through the league in Dan Casey (28–13), Charlie Buffinton (21–17), and Charlie Ferguson (his last season), who was 22–10.

Hurt by Ferguson's death in the spring of 1888, the Phillies never seriously challenged. Buffinton won 28, an impressive number, but in those years of small, strong-armed staffs, four pitchers in the league did better. The Phillies added to the staff that year a feisty right-hander named William ("Kid") Gleason. Gleason was a pitcher for his first seven big-league seasons, then switched to second base and after making a tour of several clubs later returned to the Phillies in 1903 as a second baseman. Still later he attained unwanted

Ace pitcher Charlie Buffinton (1887–1889) decided to pose with a bat.

ing in the Tri-State League who was "quite a hitter." The player's name was Ed Delahanty. Wright suggested that Reach make the deal.

So for $1,900, which for the time was a sizable amount of money for a minor leaguer, the Phillies bought twenty-year-old Ed Delahanty, the man who was to become one of baseball's all-time great hitters.

Later an outfielder, the youngster was a second baseman when he reported to the Phillies during the 1888 season. The oldest and by far most gifted of five brothers who would play in the major leagues, the right-hand–hitting Delahanty stood an inch or two under 6 feet and was of robust physique. Ed was of dual disposition, congenial, and fun loving sometimes, surly and belligerent at others, with booze the primary culprit for the transition. He liked to drink, associated with "the sporting crowd," and was known to hang his hat in the brothels that were then holding back the night on Vine and Buttonwood Streets.

Delahanty's debut in 1888 was hardly a harbinger of what was to come: In 74 games he bat-

celebrity as manager—hapless manager, one might say—of the notorious Chicago White Sox, who threw the 1919 World Series. Just twenty-one years old in his rookie season, Gleason posted an unpromising 7–16 record.

No one suspected it at the time, but in July 1888 the Phillies had made what was to prove one of their landmark acquisitions. Reach told Wright that there was a fellow playing for Wheel-

Ed Delahanty (1888–1889, 1891–1901) hit between .397 and .408 four times for the Phillies.

ted .228 and showed little extrabase power. Also, he committed 44 errors, although he did demonstrate speed of foot with 38 stolen bases.

A year later "Big Ed" was joined on the Phillies by "Big Sam." This was Sam Thompson, a 6-footer of cemented physique who in four years in the Detroit outfield had established himself as one of the league's premier busters. In 1887 Sam had led in batting (.372), runs batted in (RBIs) (166), and hits (203), amassing these statistics in just 127 games. When it folded up after the 1888 season, the Detroit club began selling its players, with Reach snaring Big Sam. In Delahanty and Thompson, the Phillies now had in place two-thirds of what many fans went to their graves swearing was the greatest of all outfields.

In his first season in Philadelphia, the Indiana-born Thompson belted a league-high 20 home runs and drove in 111 runs. Hampered by injuries, Delahanty got into just 54 games, batting .294, with no home runs. The Phillies were beginning to wonder whether Ed was going to be as good as they hoped. Manager Wright observed that Delahanty "meets the ball well, but he can't keep it away from the fielders." So, just a few years before Wee Willie Keeler uttered one of the game's undying lines in explaining his magical way at home plate, "I hit 'em where they ain't," young Ed Delahanty's problem seemed the opposite—"Hitting 'em where they was."

Outfielder Sam Thompson (1889–1898), one of the big sockers of nineteenth-century baseball.

TOWARD THE MODERN ERA

For a half dozen years the National League and American Association had been in competition with one another; then, in 1890, they were joined by a hurriedly hammered together circuit known as the Players' League. This outfit had been formed out of grievances, the chief one being that classic gripe: money. "We weren't getting our honest share," one player said, making the keynote speech for the new league. (The annual salary for most players at the time was less than $2,000.)

So the disgruntled athletes—as many as 80 percent of the National League personnel, according to one estimate—got together and organized their own league. The newcomers set up an 8-team structure, including a stop in Philadelphia, which, in addition to the American Association team, gave the city a trio of ball clubs. The Phillies lost most of their players to the upstarts, including ace pitcher Charlie Buffinton. The team managed to hold on to Sam Thompson, but in an almost comic series of checkerboard jumps, they lost Delahanty.

Big Ed originally enlisted in the new league with his mates, signing a contract. Then John Rogers, Reach's partner and a lawyer, induced Ed back with a lure of cash and a more enticing contract. At that point the agents of the Players' outfit pounced once more and talked the malleable Delahanty back onto the trampoline for a third jump, this one to the freshly anointed franchise in Cleveland, which also happened to be Big Ed's city of birth.

Thus we come to how Kid Gleason, heretofore no better than a 9-game winner in his career, in 1890 became all-conquering on the mounds of the National League, posting a thunderous 38–17 record. The Kid was a man of doughty loyalties

(ironic for a man whose team would years later swindle a World Series right out from under him), which he pronounced he owed to Harry Wright. Virtue, on this occasion, was rewarded, as a bountiful providence allowed Gleason to pitch his way through a feeble, talent-depleted league all summer and ring up his great record.

From out of the one-year defections to the Players' League came a significant windfall for the Phillies. Suddenly in need of talent with which to replace the jumpers, the club purchased outfielder Billy Hamilton from the Kansas City club of the American Association. Standing just 5 feet, 6

Billy Hamilton (1890–1895), who averaged .360 in six seasons with the Phillies.

inches, Billy was one of early baseball's memorable base-path rockets. They called him "Sliding Billy" for what seems to have been his skill at avoiding a baseman's tag, while his reputation for speed is underlined by some of his stolen base totals: 117 with Kansas City in 1889 and 102 and 115 with the Phillies the following two years, and later in his career three times greater than 90. It must be pointed out, however, that in Billy's heyday if a runner advanced an extra base on a hit (going from first to third on a single, for instance) or on an out, he was credited with a steal. This rule remained in effect until 1898, when it was changed to the rule we have today. Honest steals or not, Billy got around the bases, scoring mammoth numbers of runs, including 196 in 1894 and 166 a year later.

After the collapse of the Players' League, the other two majors extended an amnesty to the jumpers and restored them to the clubs from which they had vaulted, a gesture motivated more by necessity than magnanimity, because much of the game's talent had been involved in the one-year defection.

Among the less forgiving owners was Reach's partner, John Rogers, who wanted no part of the defectors, all of whom remained pariahs in Philadelphia with the exception of two, Jim Fogarty and Delahanty. In the case of Fogarty it was sentiment; Jim was already ill with the tuberculosis that would soon carry him off. With Delahanty it was strictly business; Rogers may have been petty but he was not stupid. Even in embryo the Delahanty talent must have been magical, for here was a fellow who had hit indifferently in two years with the Phillies, batted a respectable .298 in the Players' League and on his return to the Phillies in 1891 batted just .243. But faith was about to be rewarded.

Beginning in 1891 the club became the fourth-place Phillies, finishing in that notch for four straight years. That wasn't bad in a league that, beginning in 1892 (after the demise of the American Association) was a 12-team setup. The Philadelphia Athletics of the American Association remained in existence but the franchise was shifted to Washington, which meant that for the first time since 1883 the Phillies had the city to themselves.

Third baseman Lave Cross (1892–1897) batted .386 in the hit-happy 1894 season and didn't figure in the batting race.

The 1891 squad produced a batting champion in Hamilton (.340) as the club began its tenure in fourth place. A year later, with the folding of the American Association, many of that league's better players found employment in what was now the only major league. Among them was third baseman Lave Cross (his given name was the resonant LaFayette Napoleon Cross), who played from 1887 to 1907 and achieved a rare distinction: the only man to have played in the upholstery of four different Philadelphia major-league clubs—the Athletics of the American Association, the Philadelphia Players' League entry, the Phillies, and later with the Athletics of the brand new American League.

Another American Association refugee was pitcher Gus Weyhing, who joined the Phillies in

Pitcher Gus Weyhing (1892–1895). His 32 wins were fourth best in the league in 1892.

1892 and pitched them into fourth place with a 32–21 record (five other pitchers in the league won as many or more games). It was in 1892 that the famous Phillies outfield began to become famous: Hamilton batted .330; Thompson, .305; and Delahanty, finally beginning to decode the pitching, .306. In a league that averaged just .245 for the year, this was impressive.

A year later, in 1893, it became a hitter's ball game. Heretofore the pitcher's box had been a neighborly 50 feet away, but now it was moved back to 60 feet, 6 inches (those extra 6 inches are a result of an early mismeasurement that has never been corrected). Suddenly it began to rain base hits, the league average jumping 35 points to .280, and nowhere did it jump higher than in Philadelphia, where the Phillies led the league with a .301 average.

The Phillie outfield ran one-two-three in the batting race, Hamilton winning with .380, followed by Thompson's .370 and Delahanty's .368. Big Ed popped 19 homers to lead the league, followed by Clements, the left-hand-hitting catcher, who hit 17. Delahanty's 146 RBIs also led the league.

This lusty firepower was entertaining and the fans loved it, but the club was still welded into fourth place. There was frustration in the front office, and when this happens the manager, even one as revered as Harry Wright, had better begin packing. So remorseful did everyone feel when Wright was canned after the 1893 season a special office was created for him—chief of umpires. The old pioneer did not hold it long, dying on October 3, 1895, at the age of sixty.

The new skipper was the club's one-time shortstop, Arthur Irwin, no longer a player. What Arthur presided over in 1894 was another fourth-place slot and a dust storm of base hits that made 1893 look pale in comparison. The league averaged .309, with the Phillies leading the way with an unbelievable .349 team mark (the first-place Baltimore Orioles were next with .343; in all, eight of the twelve teams fired away at more than .300).

Right-hander Tim Keefe (1891–1893), one of the mightiest pitchers of nineteenth-century baseball, finished up his career with the Phillies.

24 Second baseman Billy Hallman (1888–1889, 1892–1897, 1901–1903), a steady .300 sticker for the Phillies in the 1890s.

The celebrated Phillies outfield was never more celebrated. At .399 Hamilton was low man, followed by Delahanty's .400 and Thompson's .404. But even these worthies were outhit by teammate Tuck Turner, another outfielder, who got into the lineup when Ed and Sam were out with injuries; getting into eighty games, Turner hit .416. (But the four Philadelphians had to look up to batting champion Hugh Duffy of Boston, who batted an ice-capped .438.) Cross hit .386, and in fact every man in the lineup was better than .300; the low man was first baseman Honest Jack Boyle (people had names like that in the 1890s), who limped in at .301.

Fourth place for this band of sockers inevitably points the finger of guilt at the pitching staff, which Jack Taylor topped at 23 wins, a figure bettered by nine other league pitchers. With the Phillies scoring 1,143 runs in 128 games—an average of almost 9 runs per game—the pitchers almost had to be creative to lose. The club ended with a 71–57 record.

In 1895 Irwin brought the Phillies in third, thanks mainly to the three battering rams in his outfield: Delahanty (.399), Thompson (.392), and Hamilton (.389). They finished runners-up in the batting race to Cleveland's Jesse Burkett, who laminated league pitching for a .423 average. In 88 games, Clements batted .394. Thompson led the league with 18 home runs and 165 RBIs in 119 games, reflecting the constant scampering of Phillies around the bases. The club again led in hitting with a .330 average and scored the most runs, 1,068 in 131 games, an average of more than 8 runs per game.

It wasn't just indifferent pitching that nestled this hard-hitting club into third place, for the club at the top of the league in those days was hard to deal with—the Baltimore Orioles, everybody's candidate for Greatest Team of All Time until the advent of Babe Ruth's 1927 New York Yankees. Managed by Ned Hanlon, the Orioles had a galaxy of stars to match anybody's in Wee Willie Keeler, John McGraw, Hughie Jennings, Joe Kelley, Wilbert Robinson, and others.

A luxuriantly mustachioed Sam Thompson.

Between 1894 and 1899 Ed Delahanty averaged .386.

In 1896 the front office decided that Irwin should be allowed to accept an offer to manage the New York Giants and that his replacement would be third baseman Billy Nash, freshly acquired from the Boston club in a trade of colossal miscalculation: the man the Phillies swapped for Nash was Hamilton, whose transgression it had been to ask Rogers for a raise. (Regrettably, it was Rogers more than Reach who was then making the executive decisions.)

Without Hamilton, and with Thompson slipping to a mere mortal's .298, the Phillies hitting cooled off considerably to .295, and the club sank to eighth place in the 12-team league. Most of the offense was named Delahanty, Big Ed batting .397, his third straight year in those ambrosial

climes, and leading the league with 126 RBIs. Ed, who still had not won a batting title despite averaging nearly .400 for those three years, saw it go this time to Burkett's .410.

Delahanty popped 13 home runs that year, four of them coming in one memorable game on July 13 at Chicago's West Side Park. Only one other man—Boston's Bobby Lowe in 1892—had ever achieved this muscular feat, and it would be another thirty-six years before it was done again, by Lou Gehrig in 1932. In an era when most home runs were hit inside the park, Delahanty astonished the crowd of 1,100 by shooting three of his homers over the fence. So remarkable was this that after the fourth homer, the Chicago pitcher, Bill ("Adonis") Terry could not help but wait at home plate to shake Big Ed's hand.

Not long after Delahanty's home-run heroics, the Phillies stumbled into an extraordinary bit of luck. The Fall River club of the New England League had an outfielder named Phil Geier who had garnered some laudatory press clippings, and the Phillies became interested. Charlie Marston, owner of the minor-league club, set a price of $1,500 on his star and the Phillies balked. After some haggling, Marston offered to throw in another of his outfielders, twenty-year-old Napoleon Lajoie, then in his first year of pro ball and after eighty games batting an extravagant .429. The deal was made.

Phil Geier came and went in a Phillies uniform without so much as a rippling of waters, but Lajoie went on to become one of baseball's benchmark names. The Phillies played the tall, handsome Rhode Island–born Frenchman at first base and in thirty-nine games he batted .328.

There was something regally aloof about the great Lajoie from the moment he entered the big leagues, an aura that emanated from his reserved personality and from the compelling grace with which he performed on a ball field. (Unfailingly, when discussing Lajoie, his contemporaries used the word *graceful* to describe the man at his work.) In an era when rookies were ignored by teammates, Lajoie by nature went his own way, seldom mixing with anyone. In a very short time he became a prince among ball players, and in the

Nap Lajoie (1896–1900), who left the Phillies to join the brand-new American League.

Catcher Ed McFarland (1897–1901), who jumped to the American League in 1902.

manner of such later royal bloods as Christy Mathewson and Joe DiMaggio, few could say they knew him well.

Despite the addition of Lajoie and the continued heavy pounding of Delahanty, the Phillies dipped to tenth place in 1897, under the managership of George Stallings, later to win fame as manager of the "Miracle Boston Braves" of 1914, who came from last place in late July to win the pennant. But all the twenty-nine-year-old Stallings could achieve in 1897 was to antagonize every player on his team. Known for his almost aristocratic demeanor away from the field, the Georgia-born Stallings demonstrated a Jekyll-Hyde personality when he put on a uniform. He derided and castigated his players in obscenity-laden tirades, to the point where even the most leather-skinned of them refused to take it anymore.

The antagonism between Stallings and his team hit the crisis point in June 1898, midway through the skipper's second year with the club. A deputation of players, led by outfielder Dick Cooley, went to Reach and Rogers and said not only could they no longer play for Stallings but that they *would* no longer play for him. Reluctantly, the owners bought up Stallings's contract and told him to get lost.

The new manager was Bill Shettsline, who had been employed as club secretary. Bill brought the placated club in sixth. Lajoie, who had played first base in 1897 and batted .363, was moved in 1898 to second base, the position at which he was to excel for the rest of his career. He batted .328 and led the league with 127 RBIs. With the pitchers finally adjusting to the extended pitching distance, averages began returning to normal, the Phillies in 1898 batting .280 and the league .271. Delahanty was at .334 and rookie outfielder Elmer Flick broke in at .313. Another rookie, left-hander Wiley Piatt, led the staff with a 24–14 record.

The 1899 edition of the Phillies reared up from

Outfielder Elmer Flick (1898–1901), a .378 hitter in 1900, and another Phillies star lost to the American League.

Left-hander Wiley Piatt (1898–1900) succumbed to American League money in 1901.

Right-hander Frank ("Red") Donahue (1898–1901) was a 21-game winner in 1901; he opted for the American League a year later.

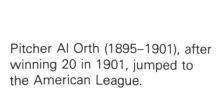

Pitcher Al Orth (1895–1901), after winning 20 in 1901, jumped to the American League.

the doldrums of the previous few years and for much of the summer put on a surprising chase for the pennant, finally settling for third place, 9 games behind the champion Brooklyn team and just 1 game behind second-place Boston. The club's 94 victories set a record for nineteenth-century Phillies teams.

Delahanty celebrated the coming end of the century by batting a rousing .408 and finally winning a batting title; he also led with 137 RBIs, 234 hits, and 56 doubles. Flick batted .342, and rookie Roy Thomas, .325. Thomas, who came right from the University of Pennsylvania campus, was to be a Phillies regular for nine years, during which he led the league in bases on balls seven times. Lajoie batted .380, but Nap missed half the season with injuries, leading Phillies fans to lament

that with a healthy Nap the team might have won the pennant.

With pitching staffs gradually expanding, the days of the thirty-five- and forty-game winners were passing, though the league did show eighteen twenty-game winners, including three from Philadelphia: Piatt (23), Red Donahue (21), and Chick Fraser (21).

In 1900 the National League contracted to 8 teams, throwing out the struggling franchises in Cleveland, Washington, Louisville, and Baltimore. Although this made the league a more wieldy structure, it also helped pave the way for the Western League—strongest of the minor leagues—to expand eastward, absorb some of the discarded franchises, and declare itself a major league. This was to prove disastrous for the Phillies.

NEW CENTURY, NEW LEAGUE

The National League played its 1900 season amid great distractions. Rumbling noises were coming from Ban Johnson's old Western League, newly christened American League. The word was that the strong-minded Johnson was going to declare his circuit a major league, refuse to recognize the reserve clause (the ball-and-chain link in every player's contract that bound his professional services to the club until it and it alone mandated otherwise), and then began raiding the National League rosters for the talent it would need for credibility.

The National League had made itself vulnerable to predators with well-nourished bank accounts, for with complete power over its players it had treated them shabbily, fining or suspending them at will, imposing a $2,400 salary cap, and otherwise behaving like a monopoly. For the National League players, the sounds rising from Ban Johnson and his well-heeled colleagues were like a circus band approaching.

The Phillies finished third again in the uneasy 1900 season, with Delahanty (.323) posted at first base that year to make way for newcomer Jimmy Slagle in the outfield. Lajoie, who had replaced Big Ed as the most popular player in town, batted .346, while Flick reached stardom with a .378 mark and league-leading 110 RBIs.

The American League opened up shop in 1901 and among its 8 newly minted big-league teams was one in Philadelphia. Making the situation rich in its complications was the fact that Ban Johnson had induced Al Reach's sporting goods partner Ben Shibe to back the new Philadelphia franchise, known by the resurrected name "Athletics." As inducement for Shibe's participation in the new enterprise, Johnson offered the sporting goods firm the contract for American League baseballs. So

when the various transactions were completed, one partner was president of the Phillies, one of the Athletics, and the American League baseballs bore the signature of Al Reach. (Owning a quarter interest in the Athletics was the club's manager, Connie Mack, beginning in 1901 what would be a 50-year tenure. Later on, he would assume majority ownership.)

The disconcerting Philadelphia crosscurrents were typical of big-league baseball's next several years. The American League's incursions on the rosters of the Nationals produced litigation, court battles, contrary decisions from different state courts, along with muttering, threats, nose-thumbing, and a general antipathy.

Some of the biggest names in the National League jumped to the Americans, among them Cy Young, Sam Crawford, Willie Keeler, John McGraw, and Jimmy Collins. With Ben Shibe's money behind him, Mack was able to induce Lajoie to join the Athletics, along with shortstop Monte Cross (no relation to Lave), and pitchers Wiley Piatt, Chick Fraser, and Bill Bernhard. (Fraser jumped back a year later.) In 1902 Flick signed with Cleveland and Delahanty with Washington, completing what was practically a complete face-lift of the Phillies roster. When a Pennsylvania court ruled that Lajoie had a valid contract with the Phillies and could not play for the Athletics, the wily Johnson finessed the ruling by shifting Nap to the Cleveland club, the Ohio courts having ruled against the reserve clause. This shenanigan led to Nap's having to skip all games in Philadelphia until the league wars came to an end a year later.

With the league in a state of confusion, the Phillies managed to place second in 1901, 7½ games behind Pittsburgh. In their final Phillie sea-

Shortstop Monte Cross (1898–1901), who left the Phillies to play for the Athletics.

summer, after some heavy drinking, he was suspended by the club. On the night of July 2, 1903, Delahanty was riding the train from Detroit to New York, still drinking. Because of some obstreperous behavior, he was put off the train at Niagara Falls. From there the story becomes murky. Delahanty evidently tried to walk across the railroad bridge and either lost his footing or jumped, plunging into the Niagara River below, where the strong currents carried him over Niagara's Horseshoe Falls. His mangled body—apparently hit by a tourist boat—was found a week later. Other versions of the tale have him being thrown from a moving train after a fight or even having committed suicide. The true story of Ed Delahanty's final living moments will probably never be known. He was thirty-five years old at the time of his death.

Not only did the Phillies finish seventh in 1902 but they also had to endure the success of the Athletics winning the American League pennant, and, worse, outdrawing the older team by

sons, Delahanty batted .357 and Flick, .336. Donahue, who jumped to the St. Louis Browns the next year, and Al Orth, who joined the Washington club, were twenty-game winners.

With their roster having been all but picked clean of stars, the Phillies finished seventh in 1902. A club that had so recently been accustomed to having clusters of .390 hitters saw outfielder Shad Barry's .287 top the team. Phillies fans couldn't help but cast wistful glances south to Washington, where Delahanty was winning the American League batting crown with a .376 average. (The first five American League batting champions were, in fact, former Phillies: Lajoie three times, Delahanty, and Flick.)

Washington fans, however, were not to be entertained for very long by Big Ed. The following

An elegantly upholstered John ("Shad") Barry, who appeared in the Phillies outfield from 1901 to 1904.

442,473 to 112,066 (it would not be until the pennant year of 1915 that the Phillies finally outdrew their neighbors).

The feuding between the leagues finally came to an end with a peace treaty in January 1903; the National League conceded full recognition to their rivals as a bona fide major league (the first World Series was played that fall). But before the pact was signed, the American League made one last foray on the Phillies roster, plucking the gifted left-hander Doc White, who signed with the Chicago White Sox, with whom he had a most successful career. Doc had been 16–20 for the seventh-place Phillies in 1902.

Early in 1903 Al Reach and John Rogers decided it was time to get out of baseball. The placid Reach and the irascible Rogers had been ill-matched in temperament but had somehow been able to work together for two decades, and although they had never won a pennant, they had done something else that in their era was even more important—they had survived, outlasting various upstart leagues and teams, remaining doggedly in place.

The club was sold to a syndicate headed by a Philadelphia socialite named James Potter, who it was said knew more about squash and indoor tennis than about baseball. (Then, as now, the chief qualification for owning a big-league baseball team is having a lot of money.)

Doing the traditional thing, new ownership fired the manager. Shettsline returned to the front office and Charles ("Chief") Zimmer took over as skipper. Zimmer was a long-time catcher, seeing most of his service with Cleveland in the 1890s. At the age of forty-three he played his last few games in a Phillies uniform.

Zimmer's reign lasted just one year, a seventh-place finish opening the trap door for him. It was a bad year all around for the club, including, on August 6, 1903, a tragedy at the Huntington Street ballpark. On that afternoon, with a ball game in progress, a fire broke out on Fifthteenth Street and a lot of people rushed up to the left field bleachers to watch it. The weight of so many people crowding at the edge cracked the rusted bolts holding together the structure and a few moments later there was the sickening sight of several hun-

dred people plunging to the street below. The final toll was eleven dead and about two hundred injured.

Phillies pitchers endured a less lethal disaster on August 27, when they issued 17 walks to the Dodgers, setting a National League record (tied by the Dodgers in 1944). (All records for individual, team, and league will hitherto date back to 1901, the beginning of what most baseball historians consider the "modern era.")

The lone bright note of the 1903 season was sounded by Chick Fraser on September 3, when he no-hit the Cubs at Chicago, 10–0.

In 1904 the National League expanded its schedule from 140 to 154 games, and this gave that year's Phillies unit the chance to be the first of many Philadelphia clubs to lose 100 games, which they did with precision, bumbling to a 54–100 record. Overseeing this trek through the wilderness was a new manager, Hugh Duffy, the same fellow who had once posted a .438 batting

Right-hander Chick Fraser (1899–1900, 1902–1904) pitched the first Phillies no-hitter of the modern era in 1903.

Hugh Duffy, Phillies manager from 1904 to 1906.

But Sherry was an outstanding player, a gift that atones for a multitude of sins.

The club also had in place the man who would put in 13 years behind the plate for them, Charles ("Red") Dooin. He had joined the Phillies in 1902 and by 1904 was the regular catcher. Red was a feisty character who became immensely popular with the hometown fans. He possessed a fine tenor voice and along with it an impish wit. He would sometimes sit on the bench and sing out his complaints to the umpire, occasionally in unflattering lyrics. When a man in blue tired of being thus serenaded he would give Red the thumb, whereupon the aggrieved Dooin would ask, "How can you throw a man out of a game for singing?"

With Dooin singing, Magee snarling, and Titus saying nothing at all, Duffy lifted the club to fourth

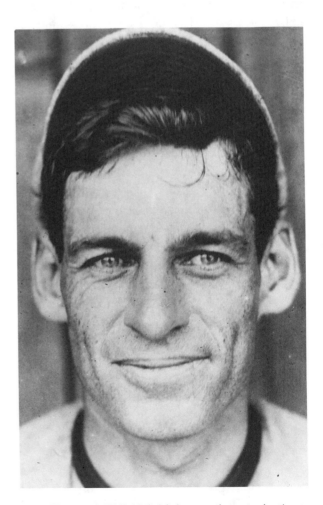

Roy Thomas, Philadelphia's steady man in the outfield from 1899 to 1908, finishing up with the club as a part-timer in 1910–1911. He was a five-time .300 hitter.

average. Hughie had no .400 stickers on his club or any .300 men either, his best men being the steady Roy Thomas (.290) and newcomer John Titus, an outfielder who batted .294. Titus's nickname was "Silent John." According to Kid Gleason, the onetime pitcher who had returned as the club's second baseman, "Titus doesn't even make any noise when he spits."

The Phillies did introduce into their lineup in 1904 twenty-year-old outfielder Sherry Magee, who would be their top hitter for the next decade. Along with his many athletic talents, Magee also brought along with him an explosive temper and a needling sarcasm that earned him the enmity of teammates, opponents, and umpires, one of whom he once decked at home plate after an argument, bringing down a fine and month-long suspension.

Outfielder "Silent John" Titus (1903–1911)

William ("Kid") Gleason pitched for the Phillies
from 1888 to 1891, then later came back as
their second baseman from 1903 to 1908.

Sherwood Magee (1904–1914), the Phillies'
best hitter through most of the century's first
decade.

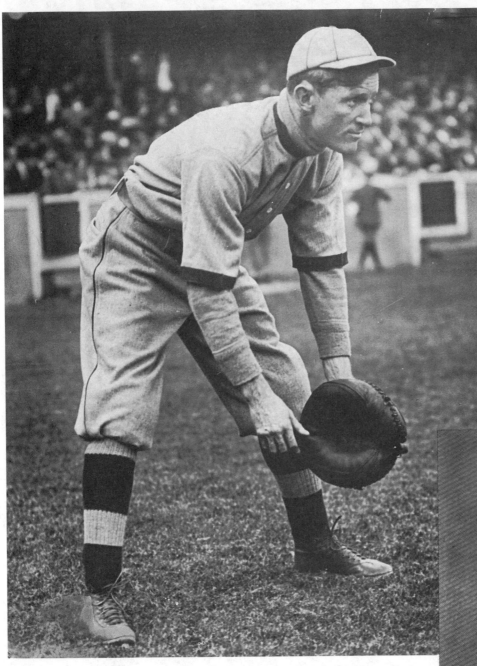

Charles ("Red") Dooin (1902–1914), the Phillies' personable catcher, who also managed the club from 1910 to 1914.

36

Charles ("Togie") Pittinger (1905–1907), who was a 23-game winner for the Phillies in 1905.

place in 1905, helped by .300 seasons from Thomas and Titus and .299 from Magee. The club was bolstered by a 23–14 record from right-hander Togie Pittinger, obtained in a trade with Pittsburgh. It was Togie's only big year for the club.

Joining the Phillies in 1905 was shortstop Mickey Doolan, by all accounts a superb glove man (these assertions are usually borne out by a woeful batting average, in Doolan's case .230 for 13 big-league years, 9 of them spent with the Phillies). Mickey hailed from Ashland, making him one of a number of Pennsylvania natives on the roster, including Magee (Clarendon), Titus (St. Clair), and Thomas (Norristown). The 1905 Phillies set the all-time club record for triples with 82.

Duffy brought the troops in for another fourth-place finish in 1906, but for a first-division club a remarkably distant 45½ games from the top, thanks to the summer's-long rampage by the Chi-

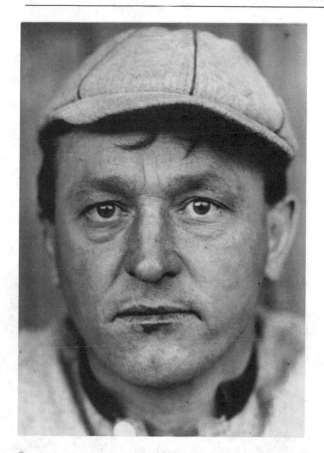

Backup catcher Fred Jacklitsch (1900–1902, 1907–1910).

cago Cubs, who won a major-league record 116 games. Left-hander Johnny Lush, out of Williamsport, Pennsylvania, gave the Phillies the game of the year with a 6–0 no-hitting of Brooklyn on May 1. Johnny was 18–15 in his first full year, although early in 1907 he was traded to the Cardinals. The top winner on the staff was right-hander Tully Sparks at 19–16.

Duffy was gone after the 1906 season, replaced by an engaging character named Billy Murray. Unlike most managers of the day, Billy had never played in the majors, having made his name as a minor-league skipper. He was a likable man, with a certain whimsical wit. Late in the season the Phillies brought up a lefty named Harry Coveleski, not without some whimsy of his own. In one of his first starts Harry had a runner reach first base. Harry paid him no mind and the man easily stole second. When Coveleski returned to the bench Murray demanded why the runner hadn't been held on.

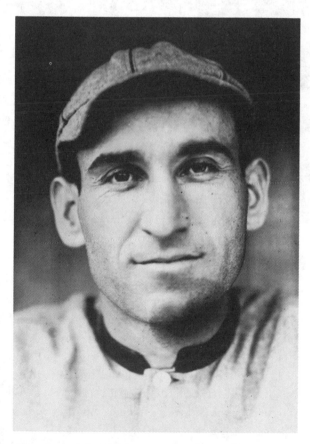

Shortstop Mickey Doolan (1905–1913), whose fine fielding compensated for his modest hitting.

Harry Coveleski (1907–1909) was called "The Giant Killer."

"I didn't know he was there," Harry quipped.

So after the game, Murray gathered his infielders and Coveleski together. Murray told the infielders that the pitcher had not known a runner was on base and then asked each the same question: "Did you know there was a runner on first and not tell Coveleski?" Each man, stifling his smile, averred that he did, whereupon the straight-faced Murray issued his injunction: "From now on, we'll have no further secrets on this club. Whenever a runner gets to base on Harry, I want you men to tell him. Understood?"

Murray's crew turned in an 83–64 record in 1907, good enough for third place. Magee's .328 average stood out among a team that batted just .236, sixth lowest in the league. It was not a year

of big bashers, attested by Magee's league-leading 85 RBIs.

The Pennsylvania connection continued with the addition of second baseman Otto Knabe (from Carrick); right-hander Lew Moren (Pittsburgh), who broke in at 11–18; and Coveleski, who hailed from Shamokin. Also joining the club at the end of the year was a hard-throwing righty named George McQuillan who started off with a 4–0 record, including three shutouts and a still-standing major-league record of 25 straight scoreless innings from the start of a career. Sparks, with a 22–8 record, was the ace in 1907.

The 1908 Phillies finished fourth, but the tail end of the season gave them, and especially Coveleski, a measure of satisfaction. Once again called

Right-hander Bill Duggleby
(1898, 1901–1907), who won
19 for the Phillies in 1901.

Ernie Courtney, who played
the infield for the Phillies
from 1905 to 1908.

Right-hander George McQuillan
(1907–1910, 1915–1916) never
came close to the 23 wins
he had in 1908.

turned in by the pitching staff—a combined earned run average of 2.10, lowest in the league. It was, of course, an era of parsimonious earned run averages, and the year the Phillies led with 2.10 the league's highest was 2.79.

In February 1909 the Phillies were sold again. The new owners were a couple of high-profile local political figures named Israel Durham and James P. McNichol, and a banker named Clarence Wolf. Durham emerged as president; his tenure, however, was short lived—he died on June 28, 1909, aged fifty-two.

It was an indifferent, fifth-place season for the Phillies, and at the end of it Billy Murray was let go. Somebody probably studied Billy's graph and detected an ominous trend: third place in 1907, fourth in 1908, fifth in 1909.

It wasn't all lemons and pickles in 1909, for the club got a fine season out of right-hander Earl Moore, formerly a star with Cleveland, who was 18–12. Lew Moren was 16–15 and McQuillan,

First baseman William ("Kitty") Bransfield (1905–1911).

up at the end of the year, Harry defeated the Giants three times in six days, helping beat John McGraw's team out of the pennant. Thereafter Harry reveled in the nickname "Giant Killer."

Murray worked McQuillan to the limit all summer, the youngster hurling 360 innings and posting a 23–17 record (because he was never the same pitcher after that, some people felt that perhaps George had been worked too hard). The club's popgun attack was led by veteran first baseman Kitty Bransfield (.304), and the boys overall hit the fewest number of home runs in Phillies history—11. Offsetting the offensive anemia were 200 stolen bases, a total no Phillies team has ever bettered. Another signal achievement this year was

Right-hander Frank Corridon (1904–1905, 1907–1909), who gave the Phillies 18 wins in 1907.

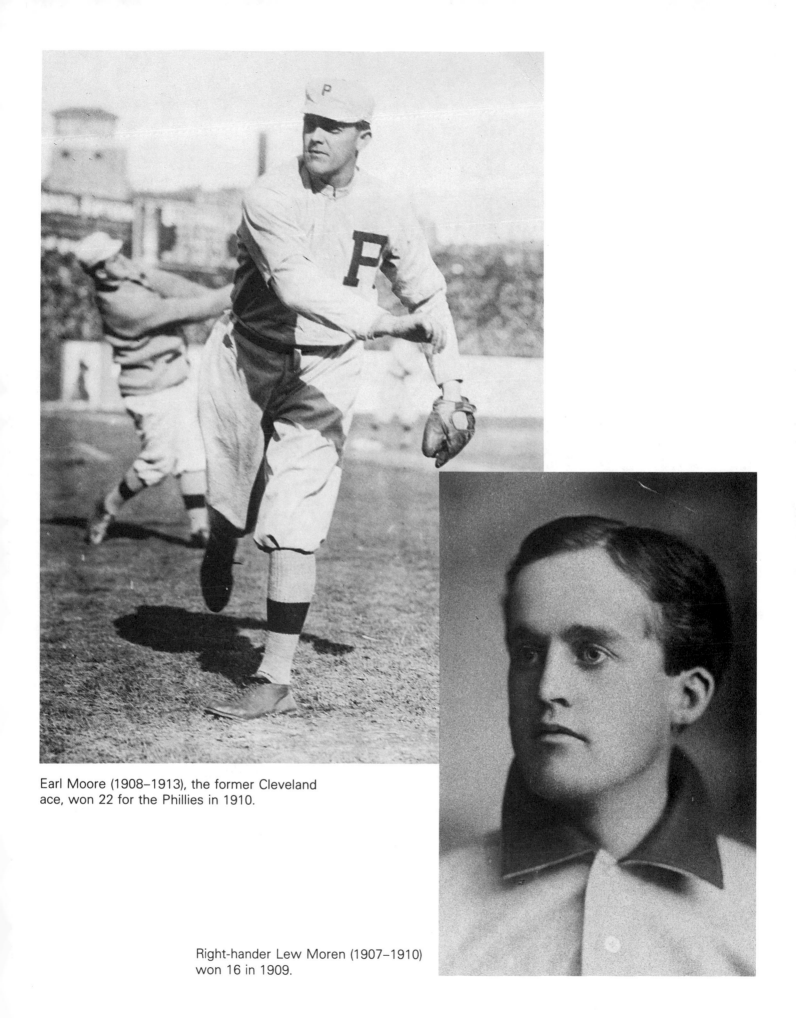

Earl Moore (1908–1913), the former Cleveland
ace, won 22 for the Phillies in 1910.

Right-hander Lew Moren (1907–1910)
won 16 in 1909.

Otto Knabe, Phillies second baseman from 1907 to 1913, when he jumped to the Federal League.

13–16. Coveleski was just 6–10 in his first full season, after which he was traded to the Reds, then flunked out of the majors until returning with Detroit in 1914 to begin three straight twenty-game seasons.

Playing third base now for the Phillies was Eddie Grant. If Eddie was an unusually thoughtful and well-spoken ball player for the time, which everyone agreed he was, it was not surprising, because he was a Harvard graduate. Eddie's major-league career was of modest distinction, ending in 1915 with the Giants. Joining the army at the outbreak of war in 1917, Eddie—Captain Edward L. Grant then—was killed in the Argonne Forest in France on October 5, 1918, just five weeks before the signing of the Armistice.

Shortly after the close of the 1909 season, Wolf and McNichol sold out their interests in the Phillies. Heading the syndicate of new owners was Philadelphia sportswriter Horace Fogel, who was installed as president. The $350,000 that it reportedly took to buy the club came from the Taft family of Cincinnati, one of whose members, the affable 300-pound William Howard Taft, was currently occupying the White House.

Fogel was a vigorous and colorful character whose résumé included not only sportswriting but also a brief stint as manager of the Giants in 1902, shortly before the 30-year tenure of John McGraw began.

With the avowed intent of injecting some "personality" into the club, Fogel hired as manager his personable catcher Red Dooin. The best Red could do, however, was a middling fourth-place finish, thanks primarily to Moore's 22–15 season (with 185 league-leading strikeouts) and 16 wins

Southpaw Ad Brennan (1910–1913) was 14–12 in 1913, his best year, after which he jumped to the Federal League.

42

Eddie Grant, Phillies third baseman from 1907 to 1910.

The grave of Eddie Grant is in the Meuse-Argonne Cemetery in France.

Bob Ewing (1910–1911) was 16–14 in 1910, his only full year with the Phillies.

from right-hander Bob Ewing, acquired from Cincinnati. (A sore arm put Bob out of business the following year.)

The most substantial day in, day out production came from Magee, who probably would have been a Most Valuable Player had the award existed then. Sherry became the club's first modern-era batting champion (.331) and also led in RBIs (123), runs (110), and slugging (.507). In addition, he was second in doubles (39) and triples (17) and stole 49 bases.

It was the club's fifth first-division finish in six years. There was nothing disgraceful in this performance, but also nothing particularly exhilarating. The Philadelphia problem lay in New York, Chicago, and Pittsburgh, whose teams had won every pennant since 1901, with the nonwinners generally occupying second or third place. Finishing fourth offered little more than mute satisfaction and sparks of hope. But help was on the way. The man who was to become the club's greatest pitcher and one of baseball's most enduring names was about to step forward.

ALEXANDER THE GREAT

The story of Grover Cleveland Alexander is one of the most poignant in baseball. A lanky, sweet-natured Nebraska farmboy who became one of the game's mightiest pitchers; who went to war in 1917 and emerged from brutal artillery barrages an epileptic and alcoholic; who in the whiskey haze of his twilight rang up baseball's most memorable strikeout (of Tony Lazzeri in the seventh game of the 1926 World Series, when Alex was a Cardinal); who left the game tied with Mathewson for National League honors at 373 victories apiece; who then drifted with aimless emptiness, his sad odyssey including a stint as a flea circus attraction on New York's Forty-second Street, and finally a lonely booze-sodden death in a furnished room back in the small-town Nebraska he had risen from.

Alexander was born on February 26, 1887, on a farm near St. Paul, a small town in the Nebraska sandhills. The tall, strong-armed, frecklefaced youngster entered pro ball with Galesburg in the Illinois-Missouri League in 1909. Midway through the season, sporting a 15–8 record, he was struck in the head by a shortstop's peg as a baserunner. When he regained consciousness two days later, he found he was suffering from double vision. Fully in the spirit of the baseball ethics of the day, Galesburg promptly sold his contract to Indianapolis, omitting the information that the young man was pitching to two batters at once. When Indianapolis realized it had been snookered, they sent Alex home and chalked it up to experience.

Sometime during the winter of 1909–1910 Alexander's vision returned to normal. This fact was not known to the Indianapolis club, whose management was a firm believer in a variant of the Golden Rule that stated "Do Unto Others as They

Grover Cleveland Alexander (1911–1917, 1930).

Have Done Unto You." In pursuance of this grim-lipped philosophy, Indianapolis sold Alex's contract to the Syracuse club, then of the New York State League, leaving out the fact that the young pitcher saw everything in duplicate. Except by now Alexander was seeing exactly what everybody else was, no more, no less. And Syracuse went

Third baseman Hans Lobert (1911–1914). His best was .327 in 1912. He managed the Phillies in 1942.

Fred Beebe. Despite histories of past success, neither Rowan nor Beebe did much for the Phillies, but Lobert and Paskert gave the club some excellent years.

Also breaking in were first baseman Fred Luderus and right-hander George Chalmers. Acquired from the Cubs the previous year, Luderus remained the regular first baseman until the end of the decade. Never a graceful fielder (one sportswriter said that Fred would have been better off carrying a prayer book than a first baseman's glove), Fred hit well and later in the decade established major-league baseball's first "iron man" record by playing in 533 consecutive games.

Alexander broke in in 1911 with the finest rookie season any pitcher has ever had: 28–13 won–lost record, 227 strikeouts, 7 shutouts, and 2.57 ERA. The smooth-working right-hander started 37 games, completed 31, and appeared 11 times in relief. His arsenal included a smoking fastball that ran in on right-handed hitters and an

from innocent dupes to possessors of treasure, baseball style.

In 1910 Alexander was 29–14 for Syracuse. If there are any doubts that talent scouting was an inexact science in baseball at the time, they are put to bed by the fact that there were no bidding wars for the services of this gifted young pitcher. After the season, Syracuse sold Alexander to the Phillies for less than $1,000.

Alex wasn't the only new face in the Phillies 1911 spring camp. In February, Fogel had traded Eddie Grant, outfielder Johnny Bates, and pitchers George McQuillan and Lew Moren to Cincinnati for third baseman Hans Lobert, outfielder Dode Paskert, and right-handers Jack Rowan and

Outfielder George ("Dode") Paskert (1911–1917) hit .315 in 1912, his top year.

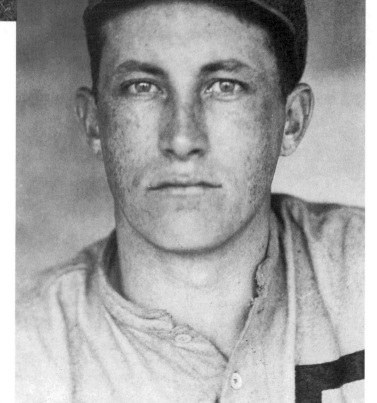

George Chalmers (1910–1916) had 13 wins in 1911, his best season. His career was ended prematurely by arm trouble.

First baseman Fred Luderus (1910–1920).

47

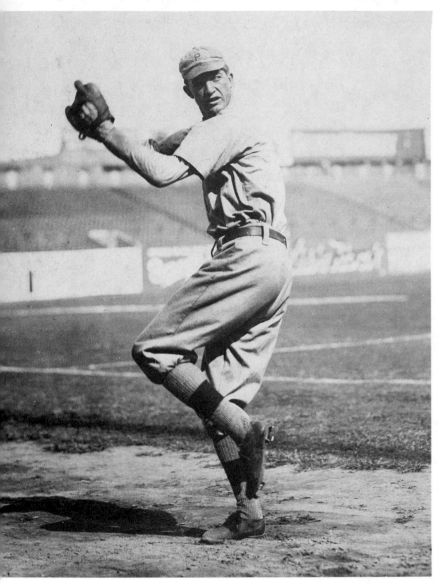

Alexander the Great. He had the greatest rookie season of any pitcher in history.

assortment of extremely sharp-breaking curves, all splendidly controlled and delivered with a deceptively effortless sidearm motion. Behind Alex, Moore was 15–19 and Chalmers, 13–10. The club finished fourth.

The 1912 season was similarly negligible, the Phillies coming in fifth. Alexander was limited to a 19–17 showing, rookie righty Tom Seaton was 16–12, and a freshman southpaw named Eppa Rixey began his Hall-of-Fame career with a 10–10 record. Tall (6 feet, 5 inches), talented, and sometimes tempestuous (especially after losing a close game), Rixey was off to a 21-year career.

Unfortunately for Phillies fans, most of that career was spent in the uniform of the Cincinnati Reds, to whom he was traded in 1921.

Another key addition to the club in 1912 was a brawny outfielder named Clifford Cravath, known as "Gavvy." Gavvy was no April daisy, having failed in previous major-league trials with the Boston Red Sox, Chicago White Sox, and Washington Senators. At the age of thirty-one, he was a well-ripened rookie. The right-hand–hitting Cravath cultivated a swing that would take advantage of the looming right field wall, which was 280 feet from home, and the right-center power alley, only 310–320 and running in an almost straight line from the foul line. These were fetching dimensions even in the dead-ball era; when the lively ball was introduced they became downright intimate. (Left field was 341 down the line and 408 in dead center.) When this Phillies ball-

Clifford ("Gavvy") Cravath (1912–1920), Philadelphia's six-time home-run leader.

park, soon to be known as Baker Bowl, is referred to as a "bandbox," it is primarily with right and right-center in mind.

With Dooin playing less and less and concentrating on managing, the Phillies began turning the catching over to young Bill Killefer, who soon developed so close a rapport with Alexander that he became the ace's favorite receiver.

"He said he felt comfortable with me behind the plate," Killefer said in later years. "He said we thought alike. Well, that was just flattery. It didn't matter what the catcher thought, or if he thought at all. Alex was going to get them out."

After the season, the team saw its president, Horace Fogel, depart. Horace, who as a former sportswriter should have known better, one day let fly some intemperate remarks to some of his old press box cronies. The gist of the remarks was: (1) that the 1912 National League pennant race was rigged, (2) that the umpires were biased in favor of the Giants, and (3) that St. Louis manager Roger Bresnahan, a former Giant, played his weakest lineup against his old team.

Fogel's remarks hit the sports pages like buckshot, infuriating league president Tom Lynch. Lynch convened a court of the seven other club presidents at a New York hotel. The opinion of this court was that Fogel had shot off his mouth to the detriment of baseball and that he should be "barred forever from the councils of the National League." (It should be pointed out that none of Fogel's charges, which he seemed to have made in a moment of pique or under the influence of liquor, were ever taken seriously.)

With Fogel having been given the boot, the Taft interests that were backing him decided to get out. In January 1913 the Phillies were sold to a syndicate headed by William H. Locke, secretary of the Pittsburgh Pirates. One of the largest investors, second only to Locke, was his cousin, William F. Baker of New York, formerly police commissioner in that city.

But Locke, who was extremely popular and who was considered an excellent baseball man, died on July 15, 1913. He was succeeded by Baker, who ran the Phillies until 1930 and whose ballpark soon became known by its most famous name, Baker Bowl.

Bill Killefer (1911–1917), Alexander's favorite catcher.

Locke's reign as club president was short, but it certainly was sweet, for in 1913 the Phillies started well and from May 4 to June 30 were in first place. Soon after, however, McGraw's Giants began steamrolling to a final 12½-game bulge over the second-place Phillies.

Aided by a livelier cork-centered ball that had been introduced in 1911 and abetted by Baker Bowl's congenial right field dimensions, Dooin's 1913 club set a new major-league home-run record of 73. Leading the troop and the league was Cravath with 19 (Gavvy also led with 128 RBIs), followed by Luderus's 18 and 11 from Magee. Cravath's .341 average placed him second in the batting race, 9 points behind Brooklyn's Jake

Roy ("Doc") Miller, a utility outfielder with the Phillies in 1912 and 1913. In 1913 he led the league with 20 pinch hits in just fifty-six at-bats.

Sherry Magee, the National League batting champion in 1910.

Outfielder Beals Becker (1913–1915), who gave the Phillies a .325 year in 1914.

Daubert. Magee was at .306 and Lobert, .300. Part-time outfielder Beals Becker, obtained from the Reds, batted .326, while Doolan and Knabe continued to flash around the middle of the infield, each leading in assists.

The ace that year was not Alexander but Seaton, who was 27–12 and the strikeout leader with 168. Alex was 22–8 with 7 shutouts, best in the league. Lefty Ad Brennan was 14–12; Rixey, 9–5; and rookie right-hander Erskine Mayer, 9–9. All around, it was a solid year for the Phillies (burnished by a new club attendance record of 470,000) and, inevitably, whetted the appetite for 1914.

The Phillies might very well have made a run for the pennant in 1914 had not war broken out—not the war that began in Europe that spring, but the one that erupted on major-league baseball. It started with the formation of a third major league, the Federal League, a jerry-built concoction foredoomed to a potter's field burial alongside the unmourned Union Association, American Association, and Players' League. True, the upstart American League had established its beachhead and succeeded; but the American League had been up against just one opponent, one that was not popular with its employees, and anyway there had been room for another league.

Foredoomed though it may have been, the Federal League nevertheless proved to be a nuisance to some teams and a headache to others. While it never achieved a successful invasion, it did making some damaging guerrilla raids on the rosters of the established leagues.

The Phillies, who had seen good teams broken apart in past baseball wars, once again were among the heavy losers. The Feds dangled some enticing long green and among the Philadelphians who leapt for it were shortstop Mickey Doolan, second baseman Otto Knabe, and pitchers Tom Seaton and Ad Brennan.

In one important respect, the Phillies were fortunate during the Federal League's shaky two-year history—the Feds did not station an outpost in Philadelphia (they did put one in Brooklyn, which meant that for two years New York had four big-league teams). Nevertheless, what had been a widely anticipated season turned into a costly di-

Tom Seaton (1912–1913), who was 27–12 in 1913, then jumped to the Federal League.

saster. Dooin's team was unable to replace its departed players adequately and finished sixth, with a drop in attendance that was commensurate with its drop in artistic fortunes—from 470,000 to 138,000.

In spite of their wretched showing in 1914, the Phillies did produce some outstanding individual years. Magee led in RBIs for the third time (103), while batting .314; Cravath, second in RBIs with 100, was again the home-run leader with 19; and Becker batted .325, second in the league by 4

Third baseman Bobby Byrne (1913–1917) had a .272 average in 1914, his best effort.

When a team drops from second place to sixth and club attendance drops by two-thirds, the manager can expect the baseball equivalent of a visitation from Marley's ghost. To no one's surprise, Dooin was given the heave-ho that fall, replaced by Pat Moran, formerly a backup catcher on the club and at the time a coach.

Moran, who had caught for the Braves and Cubs before coming to Philadelphia, was to prove an exceptionally able manager, both with the Phillies and later the Cincinnati Reds, with whom he won a pennant in 1919. Pat received high praise for his skills at running a game and for motivating his men, with whom he was generally popular. The Fitchburg, Massachusetts, native was thirty-eight years old at the time of his hiring.

Shortly after Moran's hiring, Baker dismayed many Phillies fans by selling star outfielder Sherry Magee to the Braves. The deal broke no hearts among the Philadelphia players, however, all of whom were fed up with Magee's acid disposition. To replace Magee, Baker turned some of the received cash back to Boston a few months later for outfielder George ("Possum") Whitted, hardly a player of Magee's stature but one who gave the club some surprisingly good work over the next few years.

Baker then traded Lobert to the Giants for third baseman Milt Stock, right-hander Al Demaree, and catcher Bert Adams, a deal that panned out well for the Phillies.

With Dooin still on the roster as a catcher, Baker swapped his exmanager to the Reds for second baseman Bert Niehoff. The final piece was fitted into the puzzle when the Phillies bought from the Pacific Coast League switch-hitting shortstop Dave Bancroft, soon to become one of the best and eventually to reach the Hall of Fame. The 1915 team was now set.

When it finally did arrive in 1915, the Phillies' long-awaited first pennant was won with comparative ease. After conditioning his club at St. Petersburg, Florida (the Phillies were one of the first big-league teams to train in that coastal city, then little more than a fishing village), Moran got them off to a strong start. The club was in first place from April 14 to May 21, then jockeyed between first and second with the Cubs, finally assuming permanent possession of the top rung in mid-July. The final margin was 7 games over second-place Boston. The club's won–lost record of 90–52 was modest for a pennant winner, its .592 percentage lowest of any National League winner until 1926. It was a season of parity in the league unlike any other, as testified to by the fact that the Giants, finishing last, were just 21 games from the top, their .454 percentage highest ever for a tail ender.

This was the year that Grover Cleveland Alexander truly began marching to the beat of his own drummer. Alex rang up an imposing 31–10 record, leading in wins (9 better than the next man), ERA (1.22), strikeouts (241), complete games (36), innings (376), and shutouts (12), remarkable stats for a man pitching in a "hitter's" park. When Alex wasn't winning, it was Erskine Mayer (21–15) or Al Demaree (14–11). Rixey was 11–12 and George Chalmers, recovered from several years of arm miseries, was 8–9.

Gavvy Cravath hit 24 home runs, establishing a new major-league record (it would last until 1919, when Babe Ruth popped 29 for the Red Sox), and led in RBIs with 115. Luderus batted .315, the club's only .300 man. Whitted was at .281 and the rookie Bancroft, .254.

The pennant clincher was won on September 29 in Boston with a 5–0 victory, pitched, appropriately, by Alexander. Alex did it up fine, too, spinning a 1-hitter, his fourth of the season, still the major-league record (this incomparable pitcher never threw a no-hitter).

Pat Moran, Phillies manager from 1915 to 1918.

Grover Cleveland Alexander, who from 1915 through 1917 won 94 games.

The Phillies pitchers lining up for a photograph in 1915. Left to right: Stan Baumgartner, Grover Cleveland Alexander, Ben Tincup, Erskine Mayer, Al Demaree, Joe Oeschger, George McQuillan.

While having a World Series played in their city was no novelty—Connie Mack's Athletics had brought postseason excitement to Philadelphia in 1905, 1910, 1911, 1913, and 1914—it certainly raised a high tide of excitement for Phillies fans. The opposition was provided by a pitching-rich Boston Red Sox unit, managed by Bill Carrigan. The Sox staff featured right-handers Rube Foster and Ernie Shore and lefties Dutch Leonard and twenty-year-old Babe Ruth, an 18-game winner (Ruth's only appearance in this, the first of his many World Series, was as a pinch hitter). The star of Boston's offense was center fielder Tris Speaker, part of one of baseball's finest all-around outfields that included Duffy Lewis in left and Harry Hooper in right.

The Series opened at Baker Bowl with Phillies fans sitting back and enjoying exactly what they expected—a smooth 3–1 victory delivered by Alexander.

Game 2 featured the presence of Woodrow Wilson, the first president to attend a World Series game. Wilson's late arrival delayed the start of the game by about twenty minutes, something that would surely not happen today: no president would dare be late for so august an event, and no World Series game would be held up for anything less than a beer commercial.

Game 2 began what was for Phillies fans a maddening pattern—three consecutive defeats by the same 2–1 score. It was Foster 3-hitting the Phillies in this one, beating Mayer, with Foster's own single in the top of the ninth scoring the deciding run.

Game 3, in Boston, was played not at the Sox's Fenway Park home but rather at Braves Field, home grounds of Boston's National League club, because of a much larger seating capacity (some 42,000). Back on two days' rest, Alexander pitched well, but went down by that pinchpenny 2–1 score, losing to Leonard on a Lewis single in the bottom of the ninth. Again the Phillies managed just three hits.

The next day it was Chalmers's turn to suffer the 2–1 skimming, losing to Shore, the winning run scoring on a Lewis double in the sixth. (Speaker notwithstanding, Red Sox players always considered Lewis their best money hitter.)

Gavvy Cravath (left), and Tris Speaker of the Boston Red Sox at the 1915 World Series.

The fifth and final game was played at Baker Bowl, made a bit shorter in left and center by box seats put up by Baker in order to enlarge attendance and snatch a few extra bucks. This piece of architecture came back to haunt the Phillies.

With Alexander unable to work because of an injury, Moran gave the ball to Mayer, but after some Red Sox tattoo work, Rixey took over in the third with the score 2–2, Boston's second run coming on a Hooper home run into Baker's specially made bleachers. In the fourth, Luderus put the Phillies up by a run with the team's only home run of the Series, a shot over that nearby right field fence. Another run followed and the Phillies had a 4–2 lead, which Rixey guarded until the top of the eighth. At this point Lewis poled a 2-run homer into those beckoning bleachers to tie the score. In the top of the ninth those bleachers inhaled another home-run ball, Hooper's second of the game (Harry had only 2 all year) and that was the winner: 5–4, Boston.

The press immediately put Baker and his extra

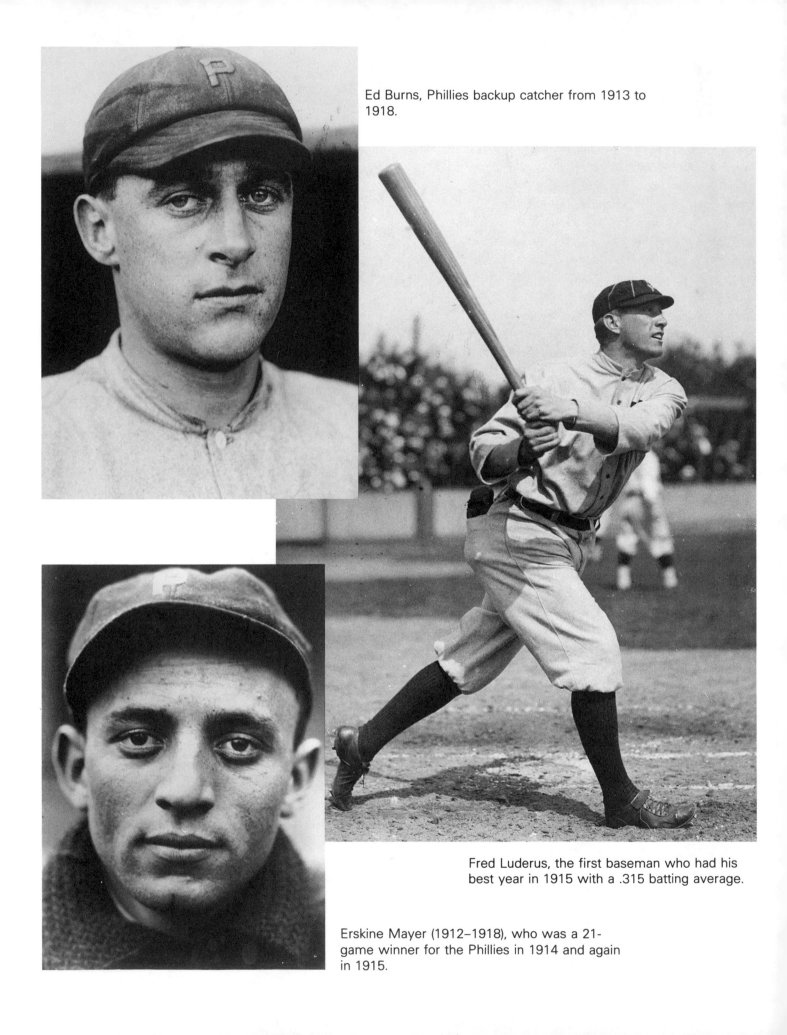

Ed Burns, Phillies backup catcher from 1913 to 1918.

Fred Luderus, the first baseman who had his best year in 1915 with a .315 batting average.

Erskine Mayer (1912–1918), who was a 21-game winner for the Phillies in 1914 and again in 1915.

The Phillies' 1916 outfield. Left to right: Gavvy Cravath, Dode Pasket, and George ("Possum") Whitted, who was with the club from 1915 to 1919.

seats on the griddle, but the fact was the same inviting target was available to the Phillies and, furthermore, the club had batted just .182 in the Series, not an average designed to win games. Luderus, with a .438 mark and 6 RBIs (of the team's 10 runs), was the only man to show a taste for that good Boston pitching. Nor could the Philadelphia pitching, holding the Sox to 12 runs in 5 games, be faulted.

In 1916 the Phillies won one more game than the previous year (91–62) and finished second. That victory total would remain the club record until 1950, while the new attendance mark of 515,365 would stand until 1946, by itself an incisive mark of Phillies fortunes.

Moran's club fought hard all summer in an all-Eastern battle with Brooklyn, Boston, and New York, finally losing out to the Dodgers by 3 games.

Three of Moran's pitchers had 74 of the club's 91 victories: Alexander (33–12), Rixey (22–10), and Demaree (19–14). The big disappointment was Mayer (7–7). Added to the staff that year was Connie Mack's former ace Chief Bender, who joined the Phillies after the demise of the Federal League, to which he had taken his fortunes. The onetime star couldn't manage better than 7–7.

For Alexander it was another season of glittering brilliance. Along with his league-leading victory total, the ace led in ERA (1.55), strikeouts (167), innings (389), complete games (38), and

57

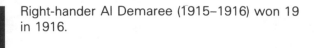

Right-hander Al Demaree (1915–1916) won 19 in 1916.

Grover Cleveland Alexander.

Third baseman Milt Stock (1915–1918). His best season in Philadelphia was .281 in 1916.

an all-time major-league record 16 shutouts, one of baseball's most majestic standards.

Strapped for effective starters and in the heat of a pennant race, Moran turned Demaree loose on an iron-man stunt against the Pirates on September 20: Al responded with 7–0 and 3–2 complete game victories. Three days later Alex duplicated the feat, beating the Reds 7–3 and 4–0 (of his 16 blankers, 5 were over the Reds).

Unheard of in today's era of the six- and seven-inning starting pitcher, the two-a-day pitcher occasionally appeared in the dead-ball days, when pitching was less stressful on the arm. Between 1901 and 1924, 14 such double efforts were turned in by National League pitchers, and between 1905 and 1926 10 by American Leaguers. Of these 24 performances, only 5 appeared in the lively ball era (after 1919).

After three straight seasons at the top, Cravath failed to lead in home runs in 1916, his 11 missing by one. Luderus, Whitted, and Stock each batted .281; Cravath, .283; and Paskert, .279. A nice consistency, but in 1916 not enough.

Eppa Rixey (1912–1917, 1919–1920), the big left-hander who won 22 for the Phillies in 1916.

By the time the 1917 baseball season began, the United States had entered World War I. While the conflict was to draw many players away from the game and into military service or to war-related industries (in 1918 the provost marshal issued a "work or fight" order, compelling draft-aged men into the military or what were regarded as essential industries), it did not impinge as heavily as World War II was to do, and in 1917 it was felt hardly at all.

Moran's Phillies got off to a good start in 1917 and as late as June 24 were in first place; soon after that, however, McGraw's Giants began pull-

Bert Adams, reserve catcher for the Phillies from 1915 to 1919.

59

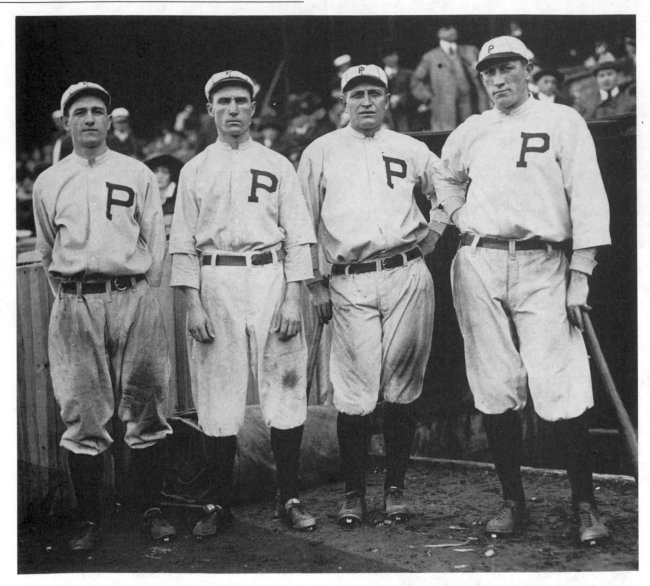

The Phillies' 1917 infield. Left to right: Milt Stock, Dave Bancroft, Bert Niehoff, and Fred Luderus.

ing away and at season's end were the winners, 10 games ahead of the second-place Phillies. First place in 1915, second for the next two years. It added up to a Golden Age in Philadelphia Phillies history. Fans then clear of eye and strong of arm would be stooped and gray-thatched before things got better.

For Grover Cleveland Alexander it was one last year of Philadelphia glory, the last of his three straight seasons of near-unassailable mound mastery. "Old Low and Away," as they called him for the sharp-breaking curveballs he delivered with such meticulous design and precision, mounted a 30–13 record, again leading in wins, innings (388), strikeouts (201), shutouts (8), ERA (1.86),

and complete games (35). His season included another iron-man performance on September 3, when he beat the Dodgers 5–0 and 9–3.

Alex was backed by Rixey (16–21), Joe Oeschger (15–14), and Mayer (11–6). Oeschger was the man who, pitching for the Braves in 1920, went the full twenty-six innings of a 1–1 tie against Brooklyn's Leon Cadore in one of history's landmark pitching duels.

Cravath regained the home-run title in 1917 (shared with New York's Dave Robertson) with 12, highlighting an otherwise indifferent Phillies attack, although the club did lead the league with 225 doubles, many of them bouncing off of that amiable wall in right field.

With real bombshells exploding in Europe, a figurative one struck in Philadelphia on December 11, 1917. After hearing that Alexander had been drafted for military service and was waiting to be called, Baker made a cold-blooded decision. Fearing that his great pitcher might not return from the smoking appetites of the cannons, the club owner sold Alex to the Cubs. War or no war, the Cubs were anxious to possess baseball's top pitcher and gave the Phillies $55,000, catcher Pickles Dillhoefer and right-hander Mike Prendergast for Alex and his steady catcher Bill Killefer. The cash was at that time the most ever involved in a player transaction.

Alexander appeared in only three games for the Cubs in 1918 before entering the army. Shipped to France with his outfit that summer, he saw considerable action on the Western Front, suffering

Grover Cleveland Alexander aboard a troop ship going to France in 1918.

through particularly savage artillery bombardments. He returned a shattered man, epileptic and alcoholic, although still an effective pitcher. He won 27 games for the Cubs in 1920 and was the ERA leader in 1919 and 1920.

Boston Red Sox fans date their club's long plunge from grace to the sale of Babe Ruth to the Yankees in January 1920, with some whimsical observers insisting that the dispatch of Ruth had the effect of placing a "curse" on the team. Well,

Joe Oeschger (1914–1919, 1924) was a 16-game winner in 1917, but then led the league with 18 losses a year later.

61

Shortstop Dave Bancroft (1915–1920).

he came to the Phillies, he had tied for the home-run lead in 1916 with 12; otherwise there was little to indicate what a buster he was soon to become.

Of all the National League clubs, the Phillies suffered least in player loss to the service or the war effort. Nevertheless, the 1918 season, which in deference to the war had been terminated at Labor Day by the provost marshal, saw the club sink to sixth place. Cravath again provided some small measure of glory, his 8 home runs giving him the lead for the fifth time in six years (with the tame ball, no one else in the league hit more than 6).

Williams batted .276 and newcomer Emil ("Irish") Meusel, brother of Bob, who starred in the Yankee outfield in the 1920s, broke in at .279. Meusel, whom the Phillies had drafted from the Pacific Coast League, was known as one of the game's toughest clutch hitters. When asked to explain Meusel's prowess under pressure, Freddie Lindstrom, later a teammate of Meusel's on the Giants, said, "It was no mystery. Irish was a dev-

if there are such malevolent agents at work in the vale of baseball, they might well have taken the sale of Alexander as a serious affront to propriety and darkened the Phillies' next three decades, for immediately after the sale of Alex, the club slipped into the longest twilight in baseball annals—14 consecutive second-division finishes, a peep into fourth place in 1932, then 16 more consecutive out-of-the-money finishes, 13 of them in seventh or eighth place. Players came and went, managers were hired and fired, the losses piled up (100 or more in a season 12 times), and tiers of empty seats gazed out on the team that writers would come to tag the "Phutile Phillies."

Two weeks after the Alexander sale, Baker swung another deal with the Cubs, this time coming out ahead. In an exchange of outfielders, the Phillies traded Dode Paskert for Cy Williams. Williams was a tall, left-handed hitter who would prove to be a premier power man in the approaching lively ball era. Thirty years old when

Second baseman Bert Niehoff (1915–1917) led the league with 42 doubles in 1916.

astating low-ball hitter. In those days, when a pitcher got in trouble they automatically began pitching low. Irish ate them alive."

The one serious loss the Phillies suffered to the armed services was Eppa Rixey; in 1918 the towering southpaw was in France. Between Rixey and Alexander, that was 46 of the 1917 victories struck from the ledgers. The best anyone on the 1918 staff could manage was 13, won by Prendergast and Bradley Hogg, each of whom faded out a year later.

The sale of Alexander hadn't sat well with Pat Moran and the skipper was vocal about it. Tired of listening to the hailstorm the deal had brought down on him, a peevish Baker canned the most successful manager the Phillies had ever had.

The new manager was "Colby Jack" Coombs, tagged after his alma mater, Colby College in Waterville, Maine. Jack had been an ace pitcher for the Athletics—a 31-game winner in 1910—and was highly respected.

Coombs, however, lasted for 62 games, only 18 of which his club won, before being fired. Jack

Emil ("Irish") Meusel (1918–1921), the Phillies' .300-hitting outfielder.

Cy Williams (1918–1930), the Phillies' big cracker throughout much of the 1920s.

was not sorry to leave; Baker had been meddling in the team's daily affairs and it had become just a matter of time before Colby Jack either resigned or was fired.

Coombs's replacement was the team's veteran slugger Gavvy Cravath, who apparently found his new responsibilities exhilarating. Playing in just 83 games in 1919, Gavvy batted .341 and hit 12 home runs, enough in that last year of the dead ball to earn him his sixth home-run title in seven years. At the age of thirty-eight, however, Gavvy's playing days were just about over.

Despite having the highest run total in the league (42), the gravitational pull of ineptitude exerted its soon-to-be familiar weight on the Phillies and deposited them in last place in 1919, a spot they would occupy 16 times in 27 years. Meusel had the squad's top batting average, .305.

Gavvy Cravath.

The problem, as it would be for years to come, lay with the pitching. The staff average of 4.17 was the second highest in the National League since 1901. Lee Meadows, a bespectacled right-hander acquired from the Cardinals in midseason, was the top winner at 8–10. Nobody else won more than 6. Rixey, back from the war, was 6–12.

The most memorable game of the year for the Phillies was the first of a doubleheader against the Giants at the Polo Grounds on September 28. According to the record books the contest was played in just fifty-one minutes, the fastest game by time in major-league history (won by the Giants by a 6–1 score).

As the decade came to a close, Phillies fans would soon have increasing reason to look back wistfully on the days when Pat Moran was manager, Alexander the Great bestrode their mound, and that lone and lonely pennant was raised.

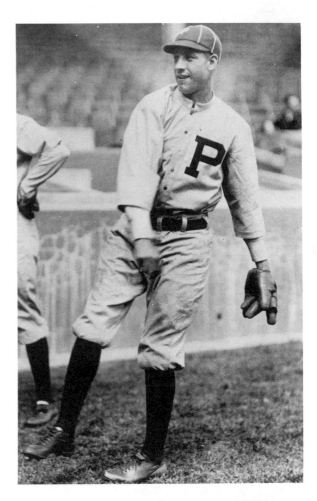

Utility infielder Harry Pearce (1917–1919).

Helping major-league baseball to try to forget the disheartening scandals of the 1919 World Series was a much livelier ball that was introduced in 1920. This new animation led to a full decade of the most prolific and thunderous hitting ever seen—a decade-long average of .285 for both leagues, punctuated by whistling line drives and home runs.

Contributing further to the disarming of the pitchers was the banning of all "trick" pitches like the spitball and other deliveries that put the ball through eccentric geometric plunges. It was also during this decade that baseballs were more frequently substituted during a game, costing the pitcher the advantages yielded by a worn or torn ball. In addition, baseballs were put into the game straight from the manufacturer's box, bright and shiny and slippery, without having been rubbed up by the umpires, as they were later to be.

So it became a hitter's game, with the Phillies participating as much as anyone else, and with that right field wall at Baker, more than most. Suddenly that 310 to 320 right-center power alley, decorated then with tin advertising signs that gave off resounding bangs when struck by line drives, was a child's-play target for the hitters. Baker Bowl became a health farm for ailing batters and a nightmare for pitchers, particularly the hometown pitchers: From 1920 through 1934, Phillies pitching staffs logged the highest earned run averages in the league.

The Phillies began baseball's new age in a prone position, looking up from eighth place with a 62–91 record, which would prove to be one of their better years of the decade. Cy Williams batted .325 and led the league with 15 homers and Meusel batted .309. The club had obtained out-

Phillies owner William Baker.

fielder Casey Stengel from the Pirates in exchange for Possum Whitted and the future legend batted .292. (A year later he was swapped to the Giants.)

Meadows survived the debacle with a 16–14 record and 2.84 ERA, which would remain the low for Phillies starters until 1943. Right-hander George Smith was 13–18 and Rixey, 11–22.

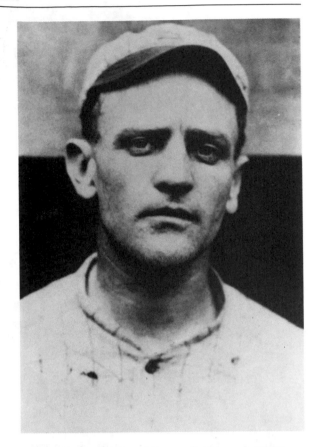

That's Charles Dillon ("Casey") Stengel, Phillies outfielder in 1920 and 1921. The future manager batted .292 in 1920 and averaged .284 over his 14-year playing career.

In June, Baker continued a pattern begun with Alexander and which was to continue in the Philadelphia front office for twenty years—he dealt away a star player. This time it was Dave Bancroft, by then one of the league's stellar shortstops. Dave was shipped to the Giants for shortstop Art Fletcher, McGraw's starter at the position for ten years but now just about through, and Bill Hubbell, a run-of-the-mill right-hander. The players Baker received were secondary to the crux of the transaction—an estimated $100,000 in cash.

Gavvy Cravath's tenure as manager came to an end with the 1920 season. He later entered politics in California and became a justice of the peace. It is assumed that in his new job Gavvy found more justice and more peace than he had as manager of the Phillies.

Succeeding Cravath was Bill Donovan, known as "Wild Bill" because of control problems early in a pitching career that had seen him star for

Brooklyn and Detroit for many years. Bill had managed the Yankees for three years without notable success. Nor did he have much success with the Phillies; after 102 games and a 31–71 record, Bill was out in the cold, replaced by another former pitcher, Irvin Wilhelm who, like everyone else at the time named Wilhelm, was nicknamed "Kaiser." It was he who shepherded the club into last place at the end of the 1921 season.

There were some new faces on the club in 1921. First baseman Gene Paulette, who had replaced Luderus in 1919, had been thrown out of baseball by Commissioner Kenesaw Mountain Landis (the game's newly installed, all-powerful czar) for associating with dubious characters. Replacing Paulette was the veteran Ed Konetchy, a 15-year veteran picked up from Brooklyn and now in his last year. Fletcher sat out the season because of deaths in his family and rookie Frank Parkinson was at shortstop. Other newcomers were third baseman–outfielder Russ Wrightstone and out-

Right-hander Lee Meadows (1919–1923), one of the Phillies' better pitchers in the early 1920s.

ght-hander George Smith
19–1922), known as
olumbia George'' for his
endance at that Ivy League
titution, led the league
h 20 losses in 1921.

The Phillies had a pitcher named Hubbell but
his first name was Bill. He worked the Baker
Bowl mound from 1920 to 1925, with 10 wins
in 1924, his best showing.

Art Fletcher, Phillies shortstop in 1920 and
1922 and manager from 1923 to 1926.

Irvin ("Kaiser") Wilhelm, Phillies manager in 1921 and 1922.

Russ Wrightstone (1920–1928). A good hitter with a leaky glove, the Phillies played him at third, first, and the outfield.

Infielder Frank Parkinson (1921–1924) struck out 93 times in 1922, most in the league and a National League record at the time.

Outfielder DeWitt Wiley LeBourveau, known as "Bevo." He was a utility player with the Phillies from 1919 to 1922.

fielder Bevo LeBourveau and pitcher Jimmy Ring. A fastballing right-hander from Maspeth, Long Island, the tough-minded Ring had been acquired from the Reds in a trade that saw Rixey go west. Ring (10–19) and Meadows (11–16) were the Phillies only double-digit winners in 1921, whereas George Smith was hammered to a 4–20 ledger, most losses in the league.

Williams batted .320 and poked 18 homers, third best in the league. But the club's other top hitter, Irish Meusel, soon went the way of so many Phillies stars. After batting .353 in 89 games, Irish

was dealt to the Giants for catcher Butch Henline, right-hander Jesse Winters, outfielder Curt Walker, and a packet estimated at $30,000.

The only satisfaction drawn by Phillies fans from the depressing 1921 season was a new National League home-run record of 88.

The 1922 Phillies caught a brief glimpse of some gray light, but only by standing on their toes, as Wilhelm got them into seventh place. The team again set a league home-run record with 116

Jimmy Ring (1921–1925, 1928), a good pitcher with a bad team. He won 18 for a last-place club in 1923.

Irish Meusel.

Walter ("Butch") Henline (1921–1926), later a
National League umpire, batted .324 in 1923.

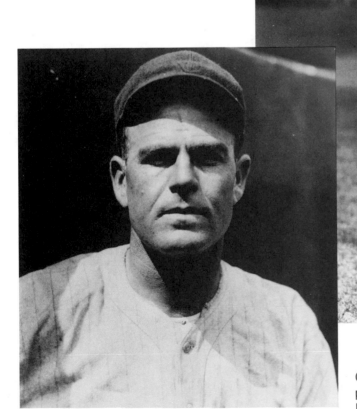

Outfielder Curt Walker hit .300 wherever he
played, and from 1921 to 1924 it was with the
Phillies, for whom he batted .337 in 1922.

ninth and had closed the gap to 26–23 before expiring with the bases loaded.

The game set still-standing records for runs in a game by both teams (49, which is 13 more than the American League record) as well as for hits in a game by both clubs (51: 26 by the Phillies, 25 by the Cubs).

Mediocre teams almost always ensure managerial changes, a baseball tradition that is some-

Cliff Lee, outfielder–first baseman with the Phillies from 1921 to 1924, during which time he batted better than .300 three times.

(it would stand for six years), with Williams leading the way with 26. Cy was one of five .300 hitters in the lineup that year, the others being Walker, Henline, Wrightstone, and outfielder Cliff Lee. Ring and Meadows each posted 12–18 records. Henline (who later became a National League umpire) made a bit of history at Baker Bowl on September 15, 1922, when he became the first National Leaguer of the modern era to hit 3 home runs in a game (Butch had 14 for the season).

The most memorable Phillies game of the season, and the game that most epitomizes the extravagant hitting of the decade, took place at Chicago's Wrigley Field on August 25. After scoring 10 runs in the bottom of the second and 14 in the bottom of the fourth, the Cubs held a 25–6 lead. But in the 1920s you were never out of a game, not when the ball had been injected with such lusty energy. The Phillies scored 3 in the top of the fifth, 8 in the eighth and 6 in the

PHILADELPHIA

	AB	R	H	PO	A	E
Wrightstone, cf	7	3	4	0	2	1
Parkinson, 2b	4	1	2	4	6	0
Williams, cf	3	1	0	2	0	0
LeBourveau, cf	4	2	3	0	0	1
Walker, rf	6	2	4	2	0	1
Mokan, lf	4	2	3	1	0	0
Fletcher, ss	3	1	0	0	2	0
J. Smith, ss	4	2	1	1	3	0
Leslie, 1b	2	1	0	4	0	0
Lee, 1b	4	4	3	6	0	1
Henline, c	2	1	2	4	0	0
Withrow, c	4	1	2	0	0	0
Ring, p	2	0	1	0	1	0
Weinert, p	4	2	1	0	0	0
a Rapp	0	0	0	0	0	0
	53	23	26	24	14	4

CHICAGO

	AB	R	H	PO	A	E
Heathcote, cf	5	5	5	4	0	1
Hollocher, ss	5	2	3	5	2	1
Kelleher, ss	1	0	0	0	2	0
Terry, 2b	5	2	2	2	2	0
Friberg, 2b	1	0	1	0	0	0
Grimes, 1b	4	2	2	7	1	0
Callaghan, rf	7	3	2	2	0	1
Miller, lf	5	3	4	1	0	0
Krug, 3b	5	4	4	1	1	1
O'Farrell, c	3	3	2	1	1	0
Hartnett, c	0	0	0	4	0	0
Kaufmann, p	2	0	0	0	1	0
b Barber	1	2	0	0	0	0
Stueland, p	1	0	0	0	0	0
c Maisel	1	0	0	0	0	0
Eubanks, p	0	0	0	0	1	0
Morris, p	0	0	0	0	0	0
Osborne, p	0	0	0	0	0	0
	46	26	25	27	9	5

(a batted for Weinert in ninth; b batted twice for Kaufmann in fourth; c batted for Stueland in seventh.)

Philadelphia	0	3	2	1	3	0	0	8	6–23
Chicago	1	10	0	14	0	1	0	0	x–26

Two-base hits—Terry, Krug (2), Mokan, Hollocher, Heathcote (2), Grimes, Withrow, Friberg, Parkinson, Walker. Three-base hits—Walker, Wrightstone. Home runs—Miller (2), O'Farrell. Sacrifice hits—Leslie, Walker, O'Farrell, Hollocher. Stolen bases—Hollocher, Weinert. Double plays—J. Smith to Parkinson to Lee. Left on base—Philadelphia 16; Chicago 9. Hits—off Kaufmann 9 in 4 innings; Stueland 7 in 3; Eubanks 3 in two-thirds inning; Morris 4 in one-third inning (none out in ninth); Osborne 3 in 1 inning; Ring 12 in 3 and one-third innings; Weinert 13 in 4 and two-thirds innings. Bases on balls—off Kaufmann 3, Ring 5, Weinert 5, Stueland 2, Eubanks 3, Morris 1, Osborne 2. Struck out—by Ring 2, Weinert 2, Stueland 1, Morris 1, Osborne 3. Hit by pitcher—by Weinert (Grimes). Wild pitch—Stueland. Winning pitcher—Kaufmann. Losing pitcher—Ring. Umpires—Hart and Rigler.

The box score for the highest-scoring game in baseball history, the Phillies versus the Cubs at Wrigley Field on August 25, 1922.

Walter ("Huck") Betts, who pitched for the Phillies from 1920 to 1925. Huck was primarily a reliever.

what akin to the search for the Fountain of Youth. So Baker fired Wilhelm and hired Art Fletcher, who had recently retired as an active player. Fletcher was a man with "a professional personality"; that is, he was a completely different character away from the field than on it. Out of uniform, Art was soft-spoken and gentlemanly; in uniform he could be, according to sportswriter Fred Lieb, "a fiend." Opponents and umpires were targets for his corrosive sarcasm and brimstone profanity. Some people attributed Art's on-the-field fury to his years under McGraw, but the truth was that Fletcher had always unleashed competitive excesses when he took to the playing field (indeed, a trait that had attracted McGraw to him in the first place).

Fletcher managed the Phillies for four years and this certainly did nothing to improve his working disposition, although Art did somehow lift the inert body of the Philadelphia Phillies to sixth place one year.

In 1923 the club found its way back to the cellar with a 50–104 record. It wasn't Williams's fault; Cy established a new club record with 41 homers, leading the league. With .300 seasons from first baseman Walter Holke (picked up from the Braves), second baseman Cotton Tierney, Henline, Cliff Lee, and outfielder Johnny Mokan, the club batted .278 but was outhit by six other teams in the league. Tierney had come from Pittsburgh (with a load of cash) for Meadows.

The departure of Meadows left Ring to labor heroically alone at the top of the staff, and the fastballer came through with his biggest season (18–16). Behind Jimmy was veteran left-hander Clarence Mitchell at 9–10. (Mitchell has his own

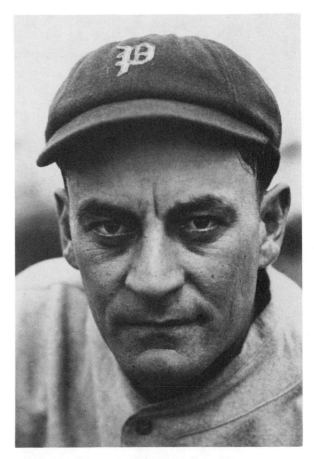

Southpaw Clarence Mitchell (1923–1928) had 10 wins in 1925, his best Philadelphia year.

special niche in baseball history: While he was pitching for the Dodgers against the Indians in the 1920 World Series he hit the line drive that second baseman Bill Wambsganss converted into an unassisted triple play.) The staff's ERA in 1923 was a bloated 5.34, at that point highest in major-league history, but like most records set in the first half of the 1920s, not destined to last very long.

Most of the excitement for Phillies fans in that season of still waters came early in the year off the home-run bat of Williams. Cy hit 3 home runs in April and then a sizzling 15 more in May, setting an as yet unbroken league record for the latter month. His 18 homers at the end of May was a league record that held fast until 1987, when Cincinnati's Eric Davis totaled 19.

A newcomer to the squad in 1923 was young catcher Jimmie Wilson, who broke into 85 games and immediately displayed the catching skills that would earn him the reputation as one of the

Catcher Jimmie Wilson (1923–1928, 1934–1938) was also the manager the second time around.

Cy Williams, the Phillies' three-time home-run leader in the 1920s.

shrewdest and best defensive catchers in National League history.

The 1924 team was spared a last-place finish only because the Boston Braves, the Phillies' chief rival for National League ineptitude during the 1920s and 1930s, landed there first. Williams was again most of the fun for Phillies fans, clearing the barriers 24 times and batting .328. Outfielder George Harper, obtained from the Reds for Curt Walker early in May, did some entertaining hitting with 16 homers and a .294 average. Holke and Wrightstone batted better than .300 and Ring and Hubbell led the staff with 10 wins apiece. Jimmy might have done even better if not for his wildness—he led the league in bases on balls for four consecutive years. Also on the staff now was veteran right-hander Hal Carlson, drafted from the minors. Carlson had pitched seven years for the Pirates, who had given up on him when he hurt his arm. But now the thirty-two-year-old pitcher

Hal Carlson (1924–1927) won 17 games in 1926.

dividing his time between first and second, batted .319 and then for some mysterious reason was sold to the minors (only to reemerge and win a batting title with Cleveland a few years later). Part-time outfielder Johnny Mokan contributed a .330 average.

The Phillies scored 812 runs in 1925, third best in the league and an average of better than 5 a game. But what the hitters (and the right field wall at Baker Ball) gaveth, the pitchers gaveth back, the staff posting a 5.02 ERA. Ring led the mound corps with a 14–16 record, followed by Carlson's 13–14 and Mitchell's 10–17. Carlson tied for the lead in shutouts with 4, which was just about as well as a pitcher could do in the batting thunder of the 1920s.

After the season Baker traded Ring to the Giants for a couple of pitchers who contributed little

Good-hitting outfielder George Harper, who was with the Phillies from 1924 to 1926. He batted .349 in 1925.

was back and in 1924 gave the Phillies some decent pitching despite an 8–17 record.

The 1925 Phillies did some lusty hitting, won 68 games (the most since 1917), and finished in a tie for sixth place. After six straight years of seventh or eighth this seemed like a genuine revival and helped nudge attendance to just over 300,000, the highest since 1920.

The club batted .295 (the league as a whole averaged .292), led by Harper's .349 (only good enough for sixth in the batting race), Williams's .331 and Wilson's .328. Wrightstone, playing infield and outfield that year, got into 92 games and swatted .346. With Holke sold to the Reds, the Phillies had a one-year wonder at first base named Louis ("Chicken") Hawks, who batted .322 and then vanished from the big leagues. Lew Fonseca,

Cy Williams (left), who could hammer a baseball, is doing
the same to his bat. A bemused Jimmy Ring is looking on.

The sun is shining brightly over Baker Bowl for this game in the early 1920s. The gentleman with the megaphone is announcing the lineups.

to the Philadelphia cause, Wayland Dean and Jack Bentley. Bentley, in fact, had a bad arm but a good bat and spent most of his one year with the Phillies playing first base before being sold back to the Giants at the end of the 1926 season.

If the Phillies seemed to have turned a corner in 1925, it only led into the blind alley of last place in 1926. The club's hitting fell to .281, 1 point better than the league average, with Williams ripping away at .345. Outfielder Freddy Leach, in his first full season, batted .329, while Wrightstone, Wilson, and Mokan were each better than .300.

Carlson gave the last-place Philadelphians a superb season, posting a 17–12 record and 3.24 ERA, which for a Baker Bowl pitcher was eye-catching. No other pitcher on the staff won in double figures.

The 1926 season marked the fourth and final year of Fletcher's managerial tenure. Art later became a long-time Yankee coach, but although frequently offered other managerial positions (including with the Yankees), his experience in Philadelphia had so soured him on the job that he was content to remain a coach for the rest of his career.

The new manager was John ("Stuffy") McInnis, former first baseman on Connie Mack's pennant-winning Athletics teams of the World War I era and member of the famous "$100,000" infield that included second baseman Eddie Collins, shortstop Jack Barry, and third baseman Frank ("Home Run") Baker. The thirty-six-year-old McInnis had just wound up a distinguished 18-year playing career.

Stuffy got into the Phillies driver's seat and immediately found that the vehicle would go only in reverse. It was a bumpy 51–103 ride into last place and after the season McInnis was canned.

The now thirty nine year old Cy Williams roused what little cheering there was at Baker Bowl in 1927 with 30 home runs (exactly half of what Babe Ruth hit for the Yankees that year), tying him with Chicago's Hack Wilson for the lead. It was the rangy Williams's fourth home-run title.

Wrightstone was the club's fourth first baseman in four years, and he came through with a .306 season, the same average as Leach. At second base the club now had the witty and personable Fresco Thompson, who batted .303. Fresco had come to the Phillies in a three-team trade that involved the Dodgers and Giants and that saw George Harper wind up with the Giants.

What little pitching McInnis had in 1927 was

Outfielder Fred Leach (1923–1928), another of the Phillies' .300-hitting outfielders in the 1920s. His best was .329 in 1926.

A glance at the Phillies bench in 1925 shows (left to right) Lew Fonseca, Jimmy Ring, Wally Kimmick, Clarence Mitchell, George Burns, and George Harper (the last man is unidentified).

John ("Stuffy") McInnis, Phillies manager in 1927.

the Phillies enjoyed a measure of what, at that point in their history, could be called success.

Shotton's tenure began with a wretched 1928 season that saw his club battered into last place with a woeful 43–109 record. With attendance averaging a little more than 2,000 per game, Baker soon began getting that empty-pocket feeling again and on May 11, 1928 felt compelled to deal away yet another of his stars. This time it was catcher Jimmie Wilson, sent to the Cardinals for catcher Spud Davis, outfielder Homer Peel, and a pile of sweet green amounting to around $30,000. While they were losing a fine all-around catcher in Wilson, in Davis the Phillies were receiving one with a considerable amount of poke in his bat (his work behind the plate was regarded as mediocre).

With Cy Williams now at the brink of retirement, the Phillies were seeking a replacement,

seriously depleted on June 27, when Baker dealt his ace Hal Carlson to the Cubs for two players and the usual cash accompaniment, this time around $50,000. Baker explained to the press that the transaction "will enable me to stay in business." This led one writer to say, "The way he said it you would have thought he was describing some blessing for Philadelphia baseball."

On November 7, 1927, Baker named Burt Shotton manager. Formerly a winged-footed outfielder with the St. Louis Browns, the forty-three-year-old Shotton, whose gentlemanly demeanor concealed a keen baseball mind, was to manage the Phillies for six years, during which time he presided over the most ferocious hitting in team history (allowing for the statistical inflations attributable to an extremely lively ball). Under Shotton,

Second baseman Fresco Thompson (1927–1930) batted .324 in 1929.

Burt Shotton (right) with Giants manager John McGraw, who is showing us his game face. Shotton managed the Phillies from 1928 to 1933.

someone with the left-handed stroke that could take advantage of that right field wall. They had heard of just such a youngster playing with the Fort Wayne club in the Central League. His name was Chuck Klein and Baker opened his wallet to the width of $5,000 to get the twenty-three-year-old outfielder, soon to become the club's greatest hitter since Delahanty.

No hitter ever took more potent advantage of Baker Bowl's nearby right field wall than Klein, a quiet man of brute physical strength. Chuck's home-park hitting during his Philadelphia years was so devastating that it ultimately earned him a place in the Hall of Fame, although some of his detractors pointed out that away from Baker Bowl he was merely better than average and not the

superstar his statistics suggested. Klein's stature as a power hitter, however, should not be penalized because he was prolific at nailing a fairly easy target. Other reputations have been similarly made—Mel Ott's at the Polo Grounds is a prominent example—and anyway, Klein's slugging was simply so staggering it cannot be ignored.

Joining the Phillies past the midseason mark, Klein got into sixty-four games and batted .360, poking 11 home runs and soon making the locals forget their decade-long hero Williams. Also entering the lineup in 1928 was third baseman Arthur ("Pinky") Whitney, who batted .301 and drove in 103 runs. Another newcomer with a smart bat was first baseman Don Hurst, who

Infielder Barney Friberg (1925–1932) batted .341 in 1930, which was sixteenth best in that year of robust hitting.

John ("Heinie") Sand, Phillies shortstop from 1923 to 1928. His best was .299 in 1927.

Chuck Klein (1928–1933, 1936–1944). Nobody ever made better use of Baker Bowl's neighborly right field wall.

Don Hurst, Phillies first baseman from 1928 to 1934.

Claude Willoughby (1925–1930), who was a 15-game winner in 1929.

Leo Sweetland (1927–1930) won 13 in 1929, his best year.

would become the club's first true regular at the position since Fred Luderus a decade before. Hurst batted .285 in his rookie year and parked 19 home runs. Sharing the catching duties with Davis was twenty-five-year-old Walt Lerian, by all accounts a splendid receiver and a .272 hitter in 1928. Sadly, his career was to be short. Soon after the 1929 season, the young man lost his life when he was struck by a truck on a street in his native Baltimore.

With 109 losses, Shotton's 1928 pitching staff didn't go home with too many high grades. Right-hander Ray Benge (8–18) was the top winner, though right-hander Claude Willoughby managed a 6–5 record. The ledger was awash with dismal won–lost records, including a 4–17 mark from one-time ace Ring, who had been reacquired; 3–15 from left-hander Les Sweetland; and an 0–12 contributed by right-hander Russ Miller in what was, understandably, his only full season in the big leagues.

So, in the light of 1928's tour of the league's nether regions, when Shotton cranked his boys up to fifth place at 71–82 in 1929, it seemed like a renaissance. The difference was, Phillies hitters began knocking in runs with almost the same extravagance that their pitchers were surrendering them. Playing with a baseball that was now almost manic in its liveliness, the National League batted .294, led by the Phillies' .309 (no team in the league batted under .280). With 153 home runs, they set a new league record (it lasted a year).

In his first full season, Klein set a new National League home-run record with 43 (it was broken a year later), batted .356, with 145 RBIs and 219 hits. Whitney batted .327, with 115 RBIs. Hurst was at .304, hit 31 homers, and drove in 125 runs. Fresco Thompson batted .324 and part-time catcher Spud Davis, .342. In early August, Hurst set a record (since broken) by hitting 6 home runs in six consecutive games. The Phillies first baseman was strictly home-run hot, because those 6 long ones were the only hits he collected over the six games.

But the biggest Phillies hitter in 1929 was not any of the above but recent arrival Frank ("Lefty") O'Doul. In one of his niftiest trades,

Lefty O'Doul, who batted .398 in 1929 and .383 in 1930, the only two years he was with the Phillies.

Baker had obtained O'Doul and twenty-five grand from the Giants in exchange for Freddy Leach. A failed left-handed pitcher who'd had trials with the Yankees and Red Sox, O'Doul was one of baseball's most personable characters as well as one of its most skilled hitters. His first full season had been 1928 with the Giants, when he batted .318. His big-league career was going to be brief— only 6 seasons in which he appeared in more than 100 games—but it was going to be lit up by a galaxy of base hits and a .349 lifetime average.

In 1929, O'Doul won the National League batting title with a gaudy .398 average. One more hit and Lefty would have been installed in baseball's throne room of .400 hitters; as it was, he whacked out 254 of them, setting the National League record (Bill Terry tied it a year later).

Among his hits were 32 home runs and he had 122 RBIs. (Interviewed years later by Lawrence Ritter for Ritter's classic *The Glory of Their Times*, O'Doul said that all that this regal pounding earned him was a $500 raise!) With O'Doul, Klein, Hurst, and Whitney each driving in 100 runs and with O'Doul, Klein, Whitney, and Thompson each collecting 200 or more hits, the Phillies set a couple of league records that are still on the books (the Cubs also had four 100-RBI men that same year).

During that hit-soaked season, the Phillies were on July 6 the victims of the heaviest scoring barrage in National League history, losing to the Cardinals, 28–6. In that game the Cardinals scored 10 runs in the first inning and again in the fifth.

The Phillies pitching staff's combined ERA of 6.13 could have qualified them for combat pay. Right-hander Claude Willoughby rode out the storm better than most, posting a 15–14 record along with a 4.99 ERA; Sweetland was 13–11 and 5.11; and Benge, 11–15 and 6.29.

But if the shell-shocked Phillies and other pitchers around the league thought that 1929 represented a hyperlively ball, a year later the hitting in the National League would pass from the staggering to the ludicrous.

MORE TOUGH GOING

The Depression that was beginning to take hold around the country did not affect the batting averages of major-league hitters, which were definitely inflationary, particularly in the National League, which outhit the American .303 to .288 and out-homered them 892 to 673.

"The ball was so lively that year," Cubs manager Joe McCarthy said, "that it seemed like we were playing in parks with 250-foot fences. It got silly after a while."

The silliness left behind hitting records that still decorate the books, some of them looking like misprints (like Hack Wilson's 190 RBIs for the Cubs, for instance, or six National League clubs batting better than .300, or seventeen players in the league driving in more than 100 runs apiece).

The Philadelphia contribution to the mayhem was considerable, with Klein doing the most notable damage. Chuck's contribution was a .386 batting average (third best in the league), 40 home runs, 250 hits, and all-time club records for doubles (59), RBIs (170), runs (158), total bases (445), and slugging (.687). With all of that, the only categories he led the league in were doubles and total bases.

The other top Phillies batting averages looked like this: O'Doul, .383; Whitney, .342; Hurst, .327; Davis, .313; utility man Barney Friberg, .341 (in 105 games); backup catcher Harry McCurdy, .331 (in 80 games); and backup first baseman Monk Sherlock, in his only big-league season, .324 (in 92 games).

Overall, the Phillies batted .315, second to the Giants' .319. Shotton's men scored 944 runs, an average of 6 per game, and still finished last with a 52–102 record. The Phillies, of course, left behind an array of all-time club records for runs, hits (1,783), singles (1,268), doubles (345), and batting average.

With a staff ERA of 6.71, the Philadelphia mound corps set the major-league record high. Somehow right-hander Phil Collins rang up a 16–11 ledger and an ERA of 4.78 which, for a man working half his games in Baker Bowl that year, was fairly impressive. Benge was 11–15 for the second year in a row, and after that it was considerably downhill, Sweetland, 7–15 and 7.71

Chuck Klein.

ERA; Willoughby, 4–17 and 7.59; Hal Elliott, 6–11 and 7.69, etc. These fellows and their colleagues gave up 1,199 opposition runs that year, still the major-league record. Those runs broke down to almost 8 per game, making the average score of a Phillies game in 1930 8–6.

Klein set a club record with a 26-game hitting streak, and in fact put together two of them; during the first, from May 18 to June 17, he was 53 for 110, a .482 batting average. Along with his many feats that year, Chuck also set a record for major-league outfielders with 44 assists, which tells you that Chuck had a good arm, that the right field wall forced him to play close to the infield, and that there were plenty of opposing baserunners doing sprints around the sacks. This latter

Lefty O'Doul.

Virgil ("Spud") Davis (1928–1933, 1938–1939), Philadelphia's good-hitting catcher, batted .349 in 1933.

Harry McCurdy (right) being interviewed in the early 1930s. A backup catcher, Harry was with the Phillies from 1930 to 1933. His 15 pinch hits led the league in 1933 (they were the only hits he had all season).

Right-hander Phil Collins (1929–1935), ''Fidgety Phil,'' was a 16-game winner in 1930.

Ray Benge (1928–1933, 1936), one of the
Phillies' more consistent starting pitchers.

88

Right-handed Hal Elliott was with the Phillies
from 1929 to 1932. Used mostly in relief, his 48
appearances in 1930 led the league.

Grover Cleveland Alexander on June 4, 1930, the day after
the Phillies released him, ending his 20-year big-league career.

image also accounts for the fact that the club was
second in double plays with 169.

"It was hard not to make double plays that
year," O'Doul said. "The other team always had
the bases loaded."

Among all the rat-a-tat-tat hitting, there was a
poignant, ghostly visitor from the past, one who
more than any other represented the antithesis of
what was happening to current-day pitching. Despite working with more than an average amount
of effectiveness, the forty-three-year-old Grover

Cleveland Alexander had been suspended by the
Cardinals late in the 1929 season for continual
relapses into drinking. After the season, in December, the Phillies acquired their onetime ace, then
but a gaunt shadow of his former self, both as
man and pitcher.

There was more than just nostalgia involved in
Alex's return to the mound where he had once
won 94 games in three years; he was now even
with Mathewson at 373 victories apiece, tops in
league history. But the old pitcher, now of wan

Arthur ("Pinky") Whitney (1928–1933, 1936–1939), the Phillies hard-hitting third baseman, batted .342 in the boom-time 1930 season.

a lot of money, which meant he had a ticket out of town. Along with Fresco Thompson, Lefty was dealt to Brooklyn for right-hander Clise Dudley and left-hander Jim ("Jumbo") Elliott, outfielder Hal Lee, and the usual envelope. After that, the Phillies sent Willoughby and shortstop Tommy Thevenow to Pittsburgh for shortstop Dick Bartell.

In Bartell the Phillies were getting a feisty, talented player—his nickname was "Rowdy Richard"—who would become a top shortstop.

Soon after completing these transactions, William Baker died unexpectedly, on December 4, 1930, at the age of sixty-four. The long-time owner's will made a rather curious disposition of his ball club. The Phillies stock was left to Mrs. Baker and to Baker's secretary, Mrs. May Mallon Nugent, with Mrs. Nugent's share being the greater.

smiles and few words, was still close to the bottle and never really gave himself a chance to nail the historic victory. He made three starts and six relief appearances, working but twenty-two innings, and was hit hard. After compiling a 0–3 record, he was released in early June, bringing to a melancholy close one of the most formidable pitching careers in big-league annals.

Soon after the close of the season Baker swung a couple of deals. O'Doul had been clamoring for more money, but at the same time he was worth

Shortstop Dick Bartell (1931–1934), twice a .300 hitter for the Phillies.

Baker Bowl from the air.

When Mrs. Baker died a few years later, her stock, too, was willed to Mrs. Nugent and her son, Gerald, Jr. This led eventually to Gerald Nugent, Sr., Baker's business manager, taking over the running of the club.

It was Nugent's fate to preside over the dreariest and most financially precarious decade in Phillies history. Baker Bowl was deteriorating and long obsolete. Fred Lieb remembered fans having to put scorecards on their heads to protect themselves from showers of rust from ancient bolts whenever a foul ball came down on the grandstand roof. Often Nugent had to borrow money to get the club to spring training and had to keep selling off star players to get the cash to meet pay-

roll and other expenses. With the season's attendance sometimes dropping to less than 200,000, it seemed at times that Nugent had more bill collectors hounding him than he had customers in his dilapidated ballpark.

Somewhat embarrassed by the animated ball they had turned loose in 1930 (and perturbed by the salary increases demanded by all of those newly minted sluggers), the baseball oligarchy put in use a more domesticated apple in 1931, and it quickly showed: The National League's average dropped from .303 to .277, its run total from 7,025 to 5,537, and its home runs from 892 to 533.

The 1931 Phillies edged into sixth place, thanks

Chuck Klein (left) and the Giants' Bill Terry. They had more than 500 hits between them in 1930.

largely to Jim Elliott, called "Jumbo" for his 6-foot, 3-inch height and 235 pounds. The big lefty was 19–14, the most wins for a Phillies pitcher since 1917. Shotton worked his ace to the limit—30 starts and 22 relief stints for a league-high 52 appearances. (In those prerelief specialist years it was common practice to employ an ace starter in relief.) Following Jumbo in the rotation were Benge (14–18) and Collins (12–16).

Klein turned in the league's heaviest hitting, leading in home runs (31) and RBIs (121), while batting .337. They might have deactivated the ball, but they hadn't pushed back the right field wall at Baker Bowl. Davis batted .326, and Buzz Arlett, who played just the one year in the majors, was at .313. Hurst and rookie second baseman Les Mallon also batted .300, helping the club to a .279 average, fourth best in the league that year.

Having sniffed the purer airs of sixth place in 1931, the Phillies went on to a surprising 78–76 fourth-place finish in 1932, thanks to the league's hardest hitting attack. The club led with a .292 average, 122 home runs, and 844 runs scored.

With the Baseball Writers of America Association having instituted a Most Valuable Player award the previous season, the winner in 1932

Don Hurst who had 143 league-leading RBIs in 1932.

James ("Jumbo") Elliott (1931–1934), whose 19 wins in 1931 topped the league.

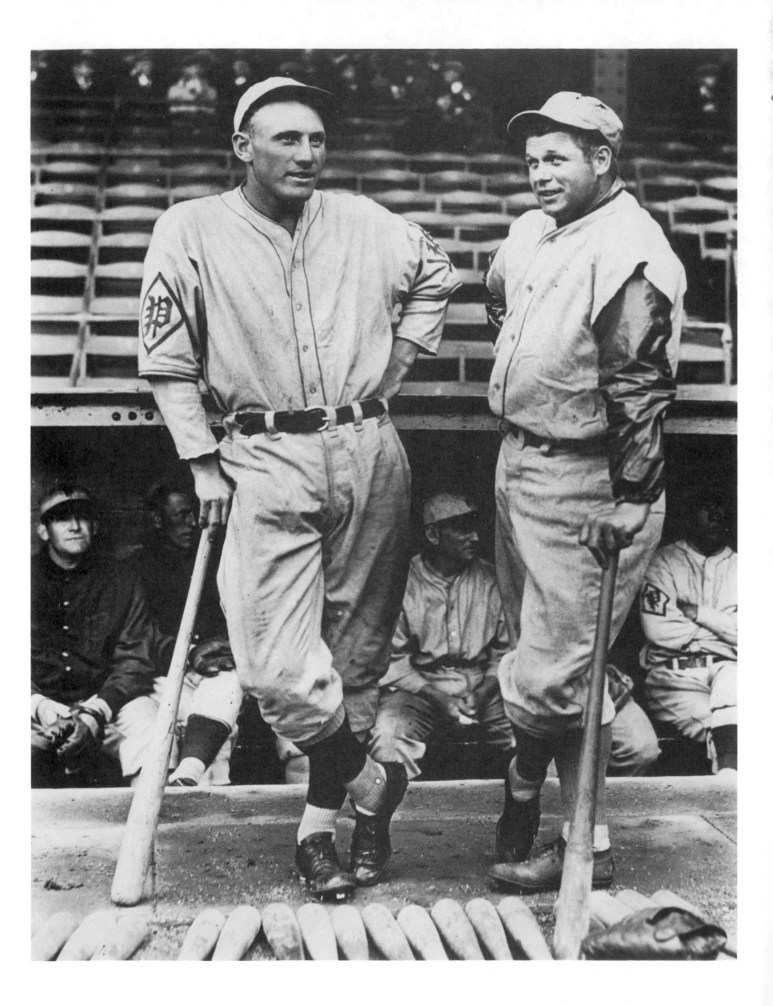

Game time at Baker Bowl in the early 1930s.

was Klein, who led the league in home runs (38), hits (226), runs (152), slugging (.646), and stolen bases (20), and he batted .348. Chuck was surrounded by smoking bats: Hurst (.339 and league-high 143 RBIs), Spud Davis (.336), outfielder Kiddo Davis (.309), Bartell (.308), and Hal Lee (.303). In Hurst, Klein (137), and Whitney (124), the Phillies had the league's top three RBI men, something no other big-league team has ever done.

This contingent of rappers helped the club to 6 double-digit winners in Collins (14–12), Benge (13–12), Jumbo Elliott (11–10), Cardinal pick-up Flint Rhem (11–7), Ed Holley (11–14), and Snipe Hansen (10–10). While the offense was scoring their 844 runs, the pitchers were helping to nullify

A couple of Philadelphia boppers: the Phillies' Chuck Klein (left) and the Athletics' Jimmie Foxx. They were each Triple Crown winners in 1933.

this largesse by yielding the league's most runs (796), although one must admit that many were unearned as the club helped undermine itself by committing the most errors, 194 (a sin the Phillies were guilty of from 1930 through 1936).

Normally, a team that has climbed from the depths to finish fourth is pervaded with an energy that compels continued improvement. Deals are made, holes in the roster are filled, progress is anticipated. Given the Phillies' thin-ice financial situation, however, the deals that Nugent made in the 1932 postseason were designed to keep the team in existence. Survival, not progress, was the focal point.

The club began by trading one of its best pitchers, Ray Benge, to the Dodgers for three players, none of whom helped the Phillies, and around $15,000. Then, in a three-way transaction with the Giants and Pirates, the Phillies gave up outfielder Kiddo Davis in return for first baseman Gus

Dugas (who did little for the Phillies) and out-fielder Chick Fullis, who gave the club a good season before being traded to St. Louis. Then, early in the 1933 season, the hard-hitting Whitney was dealt to the Braves for two players and some more sorely needed cash.

Thus punctured, the Phillies sank to seventh place in 1933 and their disheartened fans barely moved the turnstiles for an attendance of 156,000, creating further financial duress and assuring the sale of still more players.

Unfazed by the situation around him, Klein roared to yet another high-caliber season, raking

the Baker Bowl wall for a Triple Crown: .368 batting average, 28 home runs, 120 RBIs, as well as leading the league with 44 doubles, 223 hits, 365 total bases, and .602 slugging average. The club also had the league's second-best hitter in Spud Davis, who whaled away for a .349 average, one of the highest ever by a catcher. Fullis collected 200 hits and batted .309.

Right-hander Ed Holley provided Shotton with the club's best pitching, logging a 13–15 record, which meant he'd be sold to the Pirates the following summer. No other Phillies pitcher won more than 8 games.

Burt Shotton's six-year reign as Phillies manager ended with the 1933 season. With that, Nugent made a couple of other moves. In November, Spud Davis was traded to the Cardinals for ex-Phillies catcher Jimmie Wilson, whose best years were behind him. This swap reversed the one made in 1928, when Wilson had been traded to the Cardinals for Davis. Nugent, however, didn't want Wilson just to catch—which Jimmie was doing less and less of anyway—but also to manage, and duly made the appointment.

Then, on November 21, 1933, Phillies fans got the news that had seemed inevitable for several years—Chuck Klein was going and a hefty piece of change was coming. The club's greatest hitter since Delahanty was sent to the Cubs for three players of little consequence and a bag of money weighing in at $65,000.

In his five full seasons with the Phillies, Klein had whacked 200 or more hits each year, won a batting title, led in homers three times, RBIs twice, slugging three times, total bases four times, and so on and so on. But Chuck was never to enjoy the success elsewhere that he had in Philadelphia. A combination of the loss of Baker Bowl's neighborly wall and a severe leg injury reduced him from superstar to average player when he joined the Cubs.

Under Wilson, the 1934 club finished seventh, despite an influx of new talent. The belting continued at old Baker Bowl, the team averaging

Chuck Klein. The uniform was worn by National League players in the 1933 All-Star Game.

.284, third best in the league. Outfielder Johnny Moore, picked up from the Reds along with right-hander Sylvester Johnson, batted .343, and another new face in the outfield, Ethan Allen, acquired from the Cardinals, batted .330. Catcher Al Todd, Bartell, and second baseman Lou Chiozza were also over .300.

In June, Nugent made one of his best trades;

Right-hander Sylvester Johnson, who pitched in the big leagues for 19 years, from 1934 to 1940 with the Phillies.

Outfielder Ethan Allen (1934–1936) batted .330 and led the league with 42 doubles in 1934.

in a swap of first basemen, he sent the veteran Hurst to the Cubs for young Dolph Camilli. Soon to become the club's top power man, Camilli was a slugger with a fierce haymaker cut at the plate and great agility around the bag. The twenty-eight-year-old Hurst was strangely ineffective with the Cubs, batting just .199 in 51 games and then disappearing from the big-league scene.

Nugent also added some genuine talent to the staff in tall, sidewheeling right-hander Curt Davis, drafted from the Pacific Coast League. Davis, who was nicknamed "Daniel Boone" because of his sharpshooting prowess with a rifle back home in

97

Al Todd (1932–1935),
a rugged catcher, batted
.318 in 1934.

Lou Chiozza, Phillies infielder-
outfielder from 1934 to 1936.
His rookie-year average of .304
was his best.

Dolph Camilli, the Phillies'
powerhouse first baseman
from 1934 to 1937, batted
.339 in 1937.

Curt Davis (1934–1936), who broke in as a 19-game winner in 1934.

Missouri, turned in a fine 19–17 season, with a 2.96 ERA, best for a Phillies pitcher since 1920.

In June, the club bought third baseman Bucky Walters from the Red Sox. Bucky had been trying to make it as a third baseman for several years but had been just a bit light of stick; what had always impressed people, however, was his arm. "He had so much on the ball," one teammate said, "that first basemen sometimes had trouble handling his pegs." This live arm did not escape the eye of the canny Wilson, and at the end of the season he asked Walters to pitch a few innings. Reluctantly, Bucky agreed. Wilson liked what he saw and decided that come spring Walters would be a pitcher.

Bucky Walters (1934–1938), who went from mediocre third baseman to great pitcher.

After the season, Nugent again jumped into the marketplace, this time trading his fine shortstop Dick Bartell. Dick went to the Giants for four players, none of whom helped the Phillies, and a pot of cash that enabled Gerry to do his Christmas shopping and keep the store open in 1935.

The Phillies finished seventh again in 1935, spared the basement by the relentless inefficiency of the Boston Braves, who lost 115 games.

Wilson's club was in on a couple of bits of baseball history in 1935: On May 24 they participated in major-league baseball's first night game, losing

99

Jimmie Wilson, Phillies manager from 1934 to 1938.

under the lights to the Reds at Crosley Field by a 2–1 score, and a few days later, on May 30, they were the opponents of the Braves at Baker Bowl for what proved to be Babe Ruth's final major-league game, in which the sluggish, overweight, forty-year-old onetime home-run king went hitless.

"It was sad to see him struggling out there like that," Walters said of Ruth later. "Just sad."

Another player said of Ruth, "When you see Babe Ruth struggling on a ball field it makes you realize nothing lasts forever."

The Phillies staff finished seventh in the league with their 4.76 ERA. The significance of this is that it marked the only year between 1918 and 1942 that a Phillies mound corps was not last in the league in ERA.

The Philadelphia hitting in 1935 was tame compared to previous years, Moore leading the team with .323, followed by Allen's .307, with Camilli hitting 25 home runs. Davis again showed off his talents with a 16–14 record and Walters, now a full-timer on the mound, was 9–9.

After the season, the ever-agile Nugent traded his catcher Al Todd to the Pirates for catcher Earl Grace and minor-league pitcher Claude Passeau, a big right-hander who quickly developed into a first-rate starter. The Phillies, in fact, might have had their best pitching in years in Passeau, Walters, and Davis, but early in the 1936 season Nugent was back in the marketplace, swapping Davis to the Cubs. This transaction underlined the fact that Nugent was no neophyte when it came to the "trade mill." For Davis and Ethan Allen, Nugent received back Klein, another player, and $50,000. So in 1933 Nugent had been handed $65,000 for Klein and in 1936 was getting fifty grand to take him back.

Klein, however, was no longer the hitter he had been, in 117 games for the Phillies batting .309 and hitting 20 homers. Chuck did turn in one memorable day's work, on July 10, when he smashed 4 home runs in a ten-inning game against the Pirates. Adding to the satisfaction was the fact that the rare deed was accomplished not at Baker Bowl but at Forbes Field. (Chuck was the first National Leaguer since Delahanty to homer 4 times in one game.)

The star belter on the 1936 club again was Camilli, who batted .315, poled 28 homers, and drove in 102 runs. The solid-hitting Johnny Moore gave the club another good outing with a .328 average. Back again was also Pinky Whitney, reacquired from the Braves in April. Pinky had not hit very well with Boston, but Baker Bowl perked him up to close to .300.

Without the Braves cushioning them this time, the Phillies dropped into last place in 1936, with only Passeau (11–15) and Walters (11–21) winning in double figures. Bucky tied with six other pitchers for the league lead in shutouts with four.

Wilson nudged his men up to seventh place in 1937, with the club doing some heavy hitting at old Baker Bowl, now in its last full year of existence. Camilli batted .339, with 27 homers; Whit-

Earl Grace, who caught for the Phillies
in 1936 and 1937.

The talented Claude Passeau, Phillies
pitcher from 1936 to 1939.

Outfielder Johnny Moore was with the Phillies from 1934 to 1937 and batted well over .300 every year.

ney, in his last big year, batted .341; and Klein, in what was also his last truly productive season, batted .325, hitting just 15 homers, indicating that at the age of thirty-two the muscle was gone from his swing. Johnny Moore batted .319. The thirty-five-year-old Moore retired at the end of the season.

Walters was 14–15 and proving tough enough on the mound to make him a prime candidate for trading; Passeau, now a pitcher of stature, was 14–18 and was also being coveted by other clubs who, familiar with the Phillies' bottom line, were always studying the roster. A lefty named Wayne LaMaster, in his first year, was 15–19. (He was traded to the Dodgers the following year and quickly faded.) Also on the staff then was right-hander Hugh Mulcahy, who was 8–18 and soon to be tagged with one of baseball's memorable nicknames. In the box scores of the time there was a closing bit of information: losing pitcher. Mul-

cahy's name was to appear so frequently in this connection that Hughie—acknowledged as a good pitcher—became known as "Losing Pitcher" Mulcahy. (His lifetime record with the Phillies was 45–89.)

With attendance having been barely more than 200,000 in 1937, Nugent was again forced to succumb to the blandishments of his colleagues, who were by now using the Phillies as a sort of farm club. This time the man sprung from the chamber of second-division finishes was Camilli, off to the Brooklyn Dodgers, whom he was to help to a pennant with an MPV season in 1941. In return the Phillies received a player and $45,000, which helped keep the ship afloat in 1938, although the only port of call it made was last place.

The next man to leave was Walters, who was dealt to the Reds for pitcher Al Hollingsworth, one-time Phillies catcher Spud Davis, and $50,000. Bucky went on to win 49 games over the next two years and help the Reds to two pennants.

A move that had been discussed for several years could be delayed no longer. On June 30,

Right-hander Joe Bowman (1935–1936) was a 20-game loser in 1936.

Backup catcher Bill Atwood (1936–1940).

1938, the Phillies played their final game at Baker Bowl, that once proud structure which at the time of its opening in 1887 had been the paragon of ballparks, praised for its structure and appearance. But now it was antiquated and obsolete and in disrepair, victim of those most inexorable and unforgiving of agents—time and progress.

The structure stood until 1950, stringing out its years as host to circuses, carnivals, midget auto racing, miniature golf, wrestling, and whatever else might turn a buck. Today the square block bounded by Fifteenth, Huntingdon, Lehigh, and Broad is part of a commercial area, with not the slightest hint of brick or earth to show that here once prevailed Ed Delahanty and Sliding Billy Hamilton and Grover Cleveland Alexander.

Proving that sentiment lies most luxuriously in the future, only some 1,500 pallbearers showed

up to say farewell to the old park. They saw a game that had become too typically Phillies: a 14–1 loss to the Giants.

The club moved its base of operations to Shibe Park, longtime home of Connie Mack's Athletics, whose tenants they would now become. Opened in 1909, Shibe Park (in its later years known as Connie Mack Stadium) was of more orthodox dimensions than Baker Bowl had been, both along the foul lines and into the power alleys. Also, in 1939 Mack had light towers built on the park's roof, making Shibe only the third big-league park (after Cincinnati's Crosley Field and Brooklyn's Ebbets Field) to be so equipped.

Even in their worst losing years, the Phillies had been able to do some entertaining hitting, but in 1938 the bats went still. The team batted .254, second lowest in the league, and hit just 40 home

The last game at the Baker Bowl,
played on June 30, 1938.

Aerial view of Shibe Park.

Left-hander Wayne LaMaster
(1937–1938) was 15–19 in 1937,
leading the league in losses.

Right-hander Hugh Mulcahy (1935–1940, 1945–
1946) was a good pitcher with weak teams. He
led in losses in 1938 and 1940.

Del Young (1937–1940), who played
second and short for the Phillies.

Shortstop George Scharein (1937–1940).

Outfielder Herschel Martin (1937–1940).

Morrie Arnovich, Phillies outfielder from 1936 to 1940, batted .324 in 1939.

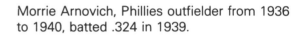

That's Morrie Arnovich hustling down the line, but Cincinnati first baseman Frank McCormick already has the ball.

A quartet of Phillies getting together in 1939. Sitting are Kirby Higbe (left) and pitcher Ray Harrell. Standing are manager Doc Prothro (left) and outfielder Joe Marty.

Chuck Klein in 1939.

signing on September 30. Jimmie moved on to Cincinnati as coach and occasional catcher and soon benefited from the acumen he had shown as Phillies manager a few years before, as Bucky Walters, the third baseman he had converted to pitcher, helped pitch the Reds and Jimmie Wilson to a couple of World Series shares.

The new manager was James ("Doc") Prothro, a successful minor-league manager and highly regarded baseball man. Prothro had had a brief big-league career as a third baseman in the 1920s, playing for the Senators, Red Sox, and Reds, 180 games in all, during which he batted .318. Doc came by his nickname legitimately—he was a graduate of the University of Tennessee dental school and for years maintained an off-season practice. He would see a lot of drilling during the season, too—of his pitchers.

Prothro's three-year tenure would result in three dismal last-place finishes, the 1939 club bumbling to a 45–106 record, including 27 losses in the month of September, tying a league record. In each of Doc's three years the Phillies would have the league's lowest batting average, score the fewest runs, and post the highest earned run average.

Arnovich batted .324 in 1939, which was as good as hanging a "For Sale" sign on him (he went to the Reds the following year). In May 1939 Passeau was traded, but again Nugent made a good deal, obtaining another future star whom he began polishing for delivery elsewhere. For their ace the Phillies received from the Cubs outfielder Joe Marty and right-handers Ray Harrell and Kirby Higbe, and $50,000. Higbe, a young, extremely hard-throwing pitcher, was the catch of the deal. The extroverted, supremely self-confident South Carolinian burned his way to a 10–14 record with the Phillies in 1939, with Mulcahy next at 9–16.

Higbe was the loser when the Phillies played the first home night game in their history, on June 1, 1939, at Shibe Park. They lost to the Pirates, 5–2.

"When I came out of the park," Higbe recalled later, "I heard some fans saying, 'That wasn't so bad. We only lost by 5–2.' That about sums up the '39 Phillies."

And the decade.

runs, figures that partially reflected the sterner dimensions of Shibe Park as well as a declining offense. Klein batted only .247 and hit 8 home runs, most on the club. First baseman Phil Weintraub, who played just the one year for the Phillies, was top hitter at .311, while outfielders Hersh Martin (.298) and Morrie Arnovich (.275) lent some respectability to the attack.

Passeau managed an 11–18 record, meaning that his Philadelphia days were running out, and Mulcahy began earning his unfortunate nickname with a 10–20 record.

The tidal waters of a 45–105 record carried Jimmie Wilson to sea with them, the skipper re-

The 1940s began for the Phillies the way the 1930s had concluded: in last place, buried under the concrete of a 50–103 record, despite the exhortations of Doc Prothro, a man who never lost his spirit or his zest.

Prothro's spirit was matched by that of young shortstop Bobby Bragan (who later did some catching), just a .222 hitter but a youngster of exuberant personality who would go on to manage at Pittsburgh, Atlanta, and Cleveland. Merrill ("Pinky") May, a .293 hitter in 1940 (highest on the club) was at third base and Johnny Rizzo, ac-

Third baseman Merrill ("Pinky") May (1939–1943) batted .293 in 1940.

Bobby Bragan (1940–1942), who caught and played shortstop for the Phillies. He later managed three big-league clubs.

quired from the Reds in June in exchange for Arnovich, was in the outfield. With 20 homers and a .292 batting average, Johnny was another of the desperate Nugent's better acquisitions. Late in the season the club brought up outfielder Danny Litwhiler, who got into 36 games and batted .345, his work including a 21-game hitting streak.

Higbe led the staff with a 14–19 record and the league with 137 strikeouts; Mulcahy was 13–22, leading in losses. No other Phillies pitcher won more than 5.

That's Bobby Bragan sliding into third with Brooklyn's Cookie Lavagetto waiting for him. The umpire looks ready with his thumb.

The club tapped away to an anemic .238 average, scoring just 494 runs as against 750 for their opponents.

After the season Nugent, whose financial situation was becoming increasingly desperate, sold Higbe to the Dodgers for $100,000 and three players. Kirby went on to win 22 games for the Dodgers in 1941 and helped the Brooks to the pennant.

The Phillies hit rock bottom in 1941 and 1942, posting records of 43–111 and 42–109, respectively, with the club's .278 winning percentage in 1942 its lowest ever. The 1941 club got some hitting from Nick Etten, a first baseman with a

good bat, who led the club with a .311 average, and from Litwhiler, who in his first full season batted .305 and launched 18 home runs. The rest of the club dwindled off to shape a .244 average. Rookie second baseman Danny Murtaugh, the future manager of the Pirates, broke into eighty-five games, batted just .219 but led the league in stolen bases with a modest 18.

Nugent never had a chance to sell Mulcahy for some needed bucks; the U.S. Army grabbed the right-hander before the start of the 1941 season, giving Hugh the distinction of being the first major-league player to go off to military service in the face of the looming war.

Philadelphia's colorful fastballer Kirby Higbe
(1939–1940).

At the top of the staff in 1941 were a couple
of twenty-one-year-old right-handers, Johnny Podgajny (9–12) and Tommy Hughes (9–14).

After three disheartening seasons of last-place
finishes, Prothro was gone. His replacement was
Hans Lobert, the club's pre–World War I third
baseman. A baseball lifer, Lobert had worked
every byway of his profession as player, coach,

scout, and minor-league manager. He was a
cheerful, friendly fellow, widely liked and respected. One player said that to forestall the theft
of his signs by the opposition, Hans had a different
set of signs for every man on the team. "How the
hell he could keep all of that sorted out in his head
is beyond me," the player said.

But no matter what signs he flashed to whom,
it all came out the same for Hans in 1942, his
club finishing last, 62½ games behind. The Phillies set an all-time record team low with 394
runs—an average of around 2½ per game—while
batting .232 (lowest in team history) and making
the most errors and posting the highest ERA.

Litwhiler's 9 home runs, 56 RBIs, and .271

Taking his rips is outfielder Danny Litwhiler
(1940–1943). Danny batted .305 in 1941, his
best year.

Shibe Park during a Phillies game in the early 1940s. In those days it was a place you visited when you wanted to be alone.

112

Veteran pitcher Silas Johnson (1940–1943, 1946).

Danny Murtaugh (1941–1943, 1946), Phillies second baseman who later became well known as manager of the Pittsburgh Pirates.

First baseman Nick Etten completing his swing. Nick (1941–1942, 1947) batted .311 in 1941. The catcher is Al Lopez.

Johnny Podgajny (1940–1943), who gave the Phillies 9 wins in 1941.

Bennie Warren, who caught for the Phillies from 1939 to 1942.

Tommy Hughes (1941–1942, 1946–1947) won 12 games in 1942, but wasn't the same pitcher when he came out of the service.

Gerry Nugent (left), the Phillies' beleaguered
owner, greeting his new skipper Hans Lobert in
1942. Hans, the club's onetime third baseman,
managed for just the one year.

115

Thompson ("Mickey") Livingston, who caught
for the Phillies from 1941 to 1943.

Power-hitting outfielder Ron Northey (1942–1944, 1946–1947, 1957) drove in 104 runs in 1944.

batting average each led the team in 1942. The Phillies added another young outfielder who would soon provide some sock—Ron Northey, a muscular left-hand hitter who possessed a particularly strong arm.

With the club losing 109 games and playing butterfinger ball in the field, Tommy Hughes's 12–18 record was something of an accomplishment in 1942. Behind Hughes was Rube Melton, a big right-hander with a smoking fastball, who was 9–20.

The following season, 1943, was one of considerable turmoil for the Phillies, who played 64–90 ball, inched into seventh place, and drew 466,975 customers, the club's best attendance figure since 1916.

In February 1943, the National League mercifully put to sleep the reign of Gerry Nugent as Phillies owner. Despite some empathy and even admiration for Nugent's decade of fingertip survival, the league had wearied of the anemic, noncompetitive Phillies teams that were circling National League parks every summer and drawing small crowds. Nugent's debts included some large ones to the league and so, after weeks of negotiations, the league took over the club. Soon after, National League president Ford Frick found a buyer for the Phillies in the person of William D. Cox.

Cox, who had made his money in the lumber business, was just thirty-three years old when he took over the Phillies. He was described as "im-

Albie Glossop, who played second for the Phillies in 1942.

patient, impetuous, and inexperienced," which sound like the ingredients for disaster. He also turned out to be meddlesome and irritating. His aggressive, impulsive approach, however, did draw new attention to the ball club and make it seem livelier, although much of the news he generated was negative.

Cox's first move was to hire the veteran Bucky Harris as manager. Bucky was the onetime "Boy Wonder," who as a twenty-seven-year-old manager–second baseman had won a pennant with Washington in 1924 and 1925. He had since managed the Red Sox and Tigers and had just completed a second term with the Senators when Cox signed him.

With wartime travel restrictions now in force, the Phillies took spring training in Hershey, Pennsylvania. Missing was Nick Etten; in one of his

Rube Melton (1941–1942) lost 20 games in 1942.

Walter ("Boom-Boom") Beck, a right-hander who pitched for the Phillies from 1939 to 1943.

final acts as owner, Nugent had dealt the first baseman to the Yankees for four players and one last check ($10,000). Also gone—to military service—were, among others, pitchers Tommy Hughes, Frank Hoerst, and Ike Pearson, infielder Emmett Mueller, and outfielder Joe Marty.

New faces included right-hander Schoolboy Rowe, former ace pitcher of the Tigers, whom Cox picked up from the Dodgers for cash; first baseman–outfielder Jimmy Wasdell, bought from Pittsburgh; first baseman–third baseman Babe Dahlgren (the man who had replaced Lou Gehrig for the Yankees in 1939), also from the Dodgers; and righty Dick Barrett, from the Cubs. Also on

117

Shibe Park.

the club that year, getting into twenty-two games, was young catcher Andy Seminick; the significance of this was that it was the first beachhead established in Philadelphia by a member of the 1950 pennant winners.

On June 1, 1943, Cox traded Litwhiler to the Cardinals, but unlike Nugent's dealings, no money was involved, the Phillies receiving in return three outfielders—Coaker Triplett, Dain Clay, and Buster Adams, the last of whom would do some solid wartime hitting for the club.

In late July the Phillies were moving along at the relative success rate of 40–53 when Harris was suddenly fired. What precipitated the dismissal was a gradual souring of relations between the overactive Cox and the more relaxed style of Harris. The owner was a frequent postgame visitor to the clubhouse (never a good idea) and would often discuss Harris's strategy with the players (a most combustible idea). Cox was genuine and in some ways successful in his desire to improve the

Left-hander Frank Hoerst. (1940–1942, 1946–1947).

118

The firing of Harris, however, set in motion a wave of events that would eventually carry Cox right out of baseball. When a still-seething Harris returned to Philadelphia after his firing, he blurted out in a meeting with newspapermen, referring to Cox, "He's a fine guy to fire me—when he gambles on games his club plays."

The reporters knew immediately that they had been handed a live grenade. When the story hit the papers a roll of thunder came immediately from the chambers of Commissioner Landis, now in the waning years of his long, autocratic service as baseball's supreme law.

Right-hander Isaac ("Ike") Pearson (1939–1942, 1946) got stuck with an 11–47 career record with the Phillies.

team, but his general approach was in inevitable conflict with that of his veteran skipper's.

Harris was fired on July 28. When the Phillies players, among whom Bucky was quite popular, heard about the canning, they threatened to strike. It was Harris himself who hosed down the uprising, pointing out that a strike wouldn't help anything or anyone.

Bucky's successor was Freddie Fitzsimmons, a longtime National League pitcher for the Giants and Dodgers, whose active career had just wound down. Fitz had a tough competitive spirit that was covered by a genial disposition. He was well liked.

Danny Litwhiler (left) and Babe Dahlgren. Dahlgren was with the Phillies in 1943.

Through it all, the Phillies had played what was for them respectable baseball (they finished seventh). Rowe was a pleasant surprise with a 14–8 record, followed by Barrett's 10–9. Left-hander Al Gerheauser, who had come in the Etten deal, was 10–19. Northey emerged as a solid hitter with 16 homers and .278 average, while Dahlgren (.287) and May (.282) topped the hitters.

Late in 1943, the Phillies were bought for an estimated $400,000 by Robert R. M. Carpenter, Sr. Carpenter was a vice-president of the gigantic du Pont Corporation and a multimillionaire. It was said that Carpenter had bought the team primarily for his son, Robert, Jr., who was more interested in professional sports than in big industry.

Robert Ruliph Morgan Carpenter, Jr., was twenty-eight years old when he became president of the Phillies. Always avidly involved in sports, he had played baseball and football at Duke Uni-

Outfielder Elvin ("Buster") Adams (1943–1945, 1947) had 109 RBIs in 1945.

Landis began an immediate investigation of Harris's charge. Cox, Harris, and others were summoned to the judge's Chicago office for a hearing. Testimony was taken from some of Cox's office help that they had, at his instructions, telephoned bookmakers for odds on Phillies games and had telephoned in his bets. The owner's only defense was that he was ignorant of baseball's antigambling statute. In other words, no real defense at all. On November 23, 1943, Landis declared Cox permanently ineligible to hold any office or employment anywhere in organized baseball.

Freddie Fitzsimmons, Phillies manager from 1943 to 1945.

versity, his alma mater. Later, he had done some sports promotion in the Wilmington, Delaware, area, concentrating on baseball, football, and boxing. At the time they bought the Phillies, the Carpenters were operating the Wilmington club in the Interstate League.

After years of stagnant ownership under Baker, and after years of Nugent's desperate struggles for survival, and after Cox's one turmoil-filled season, the Carpenters brought to the Phillies front office a substantial bankroll, a quiet dignity, and the stability that flowed therefrom. Bob Carpenter not only made the usual statements about intending to become competitive, he backed them up, which meant spending money. He was one of the early proponents of paying large signing bonuses to young prospects, a policy that was soon going to earn the club large dividends.

Shortly after he was appointed president of the

Right-hander Lynwood ("Schoolboy") Rowe (1943, 1946–1949), who gave the Phillies some winning seasons after a successful career in the American League with Detroit.

Phillies, Carpenter was notified that he would soon be called to military service. Wanting an experienced hand at the tiller in his absence, he turned to Red Sox farm director Herb Pennock—an old family friend—and offered him the general manager's job of the Phillies. With the consent of the Red Sox, Pennock, formerly an ace left-hander with the Yankees, accepted.

One thing that Carpenter and Pennock were in agreement on was that the way to success was to build from the ground up. Spending money on the purchase of a big name or two would avail them little. They were going to need a wholesale influx of talent, and this would take time. Carpenter figured that because the club had been out of the second division only once since 1918, a few more years of moldering wouldn't hurt, as long as the structuring was done effectively.

By the time the 1944 season rolled around, May, Murtaugh, and Rowe had gone off to war,

Left-hander Al Gerheauser (1943–1944) won 10 for the Phillies in 1943.

121

Phillies general manager Herb Pennock (left) at baseball's winter meetings in New York City in December 1944. National League president Ford Frick is in the center and on the right is Cincinnati Reds general manager Warren Giles.

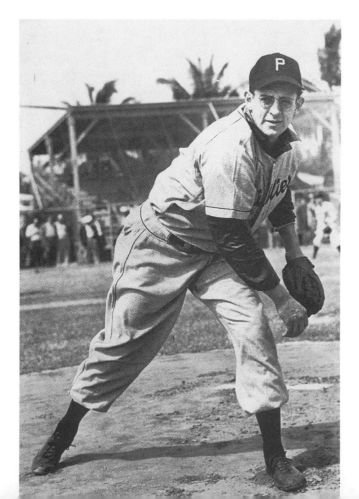

reducing even further the Phillies' talent pool. The club found its way back to last place, although not as dismally as in past years, stitching together a 61–92 record. Northey hit 22 homers and drove in 104 runs, and Buster Adams hit 17 homers and batted .283. Right-hander Charley Schanz was 13–16; Barrett, 12–18; and southpaw Ken Raffensberger, 13–20. A native of York, Pennsylvania, Raffensberger would be in the military in 1945, but soon after his return he became one of the league's most able pitchers, although most of his winning years would be spent with Cincinnati.

The 1945 season saw the club last again, this time with a dreary 46–108 record. It didn't seem to matter though; this was the summer the war ended, first in Europe in May, and then in the Pacific in August, and a spirit of relief, elation, and optimism was everywhere.

Charley Schanz pitched for the Phillies from 1944 to 1947. He won 13 in 1944, his best year.

Vince DiMaggio, shown here with brothers Joe (center) and Dominic (right).
Vince was with the Phillies in 1945 and 1946. He hit 19 homers in 1945.

With Northey in the army in 1945, the club's top power hitter was Vince DiMaggio, oldest of the three ball-playing brothers. Vince hit 19 home runs (including a team record 4 grand slams) and knocked in 84 runs. The club included another notable name in its lineup that year: Jimmie Foxx. The former American League home-run king was just hanging on now, keeping a roster spot warm until the regulars returned. Jimmie did a little of this and a little of that; playing first, second, third, pinch-hitting, and even did some pitching. He wound up in eighty-nine games, hitting 7 homers (the last of his 534 career shots) and batting .268.

Right-handed reliever Andy Karl appeared in sixty-seven games, most in the league and a high total for the time. His 8 wins tied Barrett (8–20) for most on the team.

Ken Raffensberger (1943–1947) led the league with 20 losses in 1944. The talented lefty did his best pitching for the Reds after he left the Phillies.

Jimmie Foxx, the all-time great power hitter, finished up his career with the Phillies in 1945.

Freddie Fitzsimmons had tried his best with the talent given him, which was pretty ragtag even by wartime standards. But on June 30, 1945, Fitz was left behind when the train left the station and the new skipper was Ben Chapman.

Chapman had been a swift-footed star outfielder in the American League, beginning his major-league career with the Yankees in 1930 and subsequently playing with Washington, Boston, Cleveland, and Chicago before coming to the National League with the Dodgers in 1944, from whom the Phillies got him just a few weeks before naming him manager.

One of the reasons Ben had been traded so often was his sharp tongue. Joe McCarthy, the Yankee manager who could handle "anybody" couldn't handle Ben and traded him. When he was with the Red Sox Ben ignored a bunt sign from manager Joe Cronin and then promptly banged into a double play. When confronted by an irate Cronin, Ben told the skipper, "I don't bunt." And so on. Today Chapman is probably most remembered for the racial vituperation he hurled upon Jackie Robinson when the Dodger player was attempting to make good as major-league baseball's first black player in 1947. The Southern-born Chapman always maintained that what he said was in the good old tradition of welcoming a rookie with some vocal sandpaper, but others said there was nothing "traditional" about it.

Among the players Ben led into last place in 1945 was an eighteen-year-old shortstop named Granny Hamner (he had played a few games the year before), who got into fourteen games before entering the service. Destined to become one of the fine shortstops in Phillies history, Hamner was the second member of the 1950 pennant winners to join the club, along with Andy Seminick, who was now doing most of the catching.

Right-hander Anton Karl (1943–1946), who gave the Phillies some first-class relief pitching.

ROUSING FROM HIBERNATION

The war was over, the stars were back, and the fans came flooding to the ballparks. In 1946 they came to Shibe Park in startlingly record numbers—1,045,247—more than doubling the Phillies' old attendance record set by Pat Moran's 1916 club.

The 1946 Phillies were peppered with good veteran players turned loose by the influx of returning talent and Chapman's club played a snappy, competitive game not seen by Phillies fans in years. The club finished fifth—their highest nesting since 1932—and throughout the year they were a tough outfit to beat. Shibe Park was no longer a day at the beach for visiting National League teams.

Veteran Cincinnati first baseman Frank Mc-Cormick, picked up from the Reds for $30,000, batted .284 and made just one error all year. At second was Emil Verban, from the Cardinals; at short was thirty-five-year-old Skeeter Newsome and at third Jim Tabor, both late of the Boston Red Sox. These men, admittedly past their primes, were manning the barricades until Carpenter and Pennock could begin filtering younger talent into the lineup.

One of those youngsters was already emphatically present. His name was Del Ennis, a power hitter whom the Phillies had signed right out of Philadelphia's Olney High School. After spending 1943 in the minors, Del had gone into the service, been discharged, come to spring training in 1946, and won a job. The twenty-one-year-old Ennis hit 17 home runs and batted .313, impressing everyone around the league with his right-handed power swing. Joining Ennis in the outfield were Ron Northey and Johnny Wyrostek, and with Seminick a bull behind the plate, the club had eight regulars

Veteran Frank McCormick, who filled in at first base for the Phillies in 1946–1947.

getting into more than 100 games apiece for the first time since 1940.

The veteran Rowe, back from the service, topped a mediocre staff with a 11–4 record. Lefty Oscar Judd, another pickup from the Red Sox,

Four members of the 1946 Phillies. Left to right: Ron Northey, shortstop Lamar ("Skeeter") Newsome (1946–1947), second baseman Emil Verban (1946–1948), and third baseman Jim Tabor (1946–1947).

was 11–12. No other pitcher won in double figures. Back from the war were pitchers Tommy Hughes and Hugh Mulcahy, but somewhere along the line in those dark years they had lost their fastballs.

The 1947 Phillies were unable to maintain the pace of progress, slipping back to seventh place with a 62–82 record; nevertheless, attendance remained good—907,332.

The club made a solid trade early in the season, swapping Northey to the Cardinals for outfielder

Philadelphia native Del Ennis (1946–1956), one of the great power hitters in Phillies history.

Andy Seminick (left) and veteran catcher Rollie Hemsley. Seminick caught for the Phillies from 1943 to 1951 and from 1955 to 1957. Hemsley was with the club in 1946 and 1947, when he wound up his 19-year career.

Outfielder Johnny Wyrostek (1946–1947, 1952–1954) gave the Phillies a .281 year in 1946.

Harry Walker (1947–1948), the National League batting champion in 1947.

Harry ("The Hat") Walker, so nicknamed for his habit of fidgeting with his cap between pitches. After batting .200 in 10 games with the Cardinals, Harry banged out a .371 average for the Phillies, his overall .363 mark leading the league, giving the club its first batting champ since O'Doul in 1929. Harry was also the first National Leaguer to win the title while playing with two clubs in a season. (Dale Alexander had done it in the American League in 1932, playing for Detroit and Boston.)

128

Outside of Walker, the attack was rather lame that year, Verban batting .285, while Ennis tagged just 12 homers and Seminick, 13. Former American Leaguer Dutch Leonard emerged, at the age of thirty-eight, to knuckleball his way to a 17–12 record, while Rowe was 14–10.

But help was on the way. The farm system was in the process of polishing up such youngsters as third baseman Willie ("Puddin' Head") Jones—the Mark Twain-ish nickname originated in childhood—center fielder Richie Ashburn, and Granny Hamner; in addition, the club had poured $65,000 worth of bonus money on a smoke-throwing eighteen-year-old left-hander from Egypt, Pennsylvania, named Curt Simmons. After spending the 1947 season with Wilmington, Simmons joined the Phillies and pitched the year's final game. The teenager was dazzling, 5-hitting the Giants and fanning 9 in a 3–1 victory. Despite that harbinger, the Simmons investment would be slow to pay off, but when it did, the dividends were handsome.

The Phillies signed another young pitcher that September, a right-hander who had pitched

Andy Seminick.

Emil ("Dutch") Leonard, a long-time American League right-hander, won 17 for the Phillies in 1947.

Roberts. "It was so smooth and easy. He wound up slowly, like he was out there playing catch with his grandfather, then rocked back gently, then came forward with such fluid ease—and wham! The next thing you knew he'd fired a B-B right across the knees."

The Roberts formula, as enunciated by one of his managers, was "speed, control, stamina, and guts." The speaker was Eddie Sawyer, a chief beneficiary of those combined qualities. Roberts's control enabled him to throw fewer pitches in a game, and because he worked quickly and walked so few men, his fielders were always poised and alert behind him and consequently gave him a better defense. Because he often worked a game with fewer than 100 pitches and delivered with that smoothly flowing motion, Roberts was able to pitch sizable amounts of innings—seven years in a row of 297 or more—leading the league in starts six straight times and leading in complete games

college-league ball in Vermont and who had been scouted by five clubs other than the Phillies. In September he was traveling around the country in response to invitations from these teams to work out with them. The Phillies, in Chicago at the time, happened to be the first.

After watching him work out, the Phillies offered him $10,000 to sign. The youngster, who had expected perhaps a thousand or two, demurred, although not in hopes of coaxing out more money but because "I felt a loyalty to my promise to work out with the other clubs." The next day the Phillies offered him $15,000. Still loyal, he was, he said, "Loosening up now." The third day they raised the bonus to $25,000, and Robin Roberts could no longer resist. The twenty-one-year-old young man from Springfield, Illinois, took the money and with it bought his mother a house. So Mrs. Roberts had a house and the Philadelphia Phillies had their greatest pitcher since Grover Cleveland Alexander.

"It was his motion," one Phillies coach said of

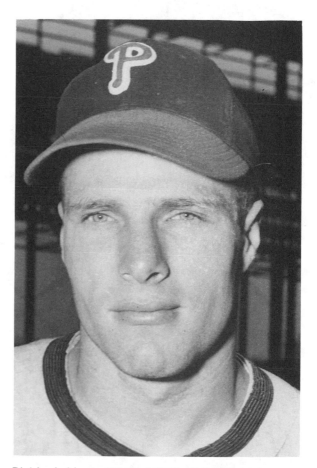

Richie Ashburn (1948–1959), Philadelphia's two-time batting champion.

Robin Roberts (1948–1961), the Phillies'
greatest pitcher since Alexander.

Curt Simmons (1947–1950, 1952–1960),
a bonus baby who paid off.

Ben Chapman (left) and Eddie Miller posing with Bob Carpenter in
the spring of 1947. Chapman managed the club from 1945 to 1948.

and innings five straight times each. As far as his
strength under pressure was concerned, it was
summed up by Sawyer, who said, "If my life de-
pended on one game, Roberts is the man I'd want
to pitch it." And when a game of this magnitude
did occur at the end of the 1950 season (some
still say it remains the single most memorable
game in Phillies history), Roberts was indeed the
man Sawyer sent to the mound.

The husky, easy-going but intensely competitive Roberts began the 1948 season at Wilmington, posted a 9–1 record and was called up in
June to begin the career that would end in the
Hall of Fame.

Roberts was one of the last acquisitions made
by Herb Pennock, for in late January 1948 the
GM died suddenly while in New York to attend
some major-league meetings. Instead of hiring a
replacement, Carpenter decided to assume the
general manager's responsibilities himself.

On April 7, 1948, Carpenter made a little-
noticed transaction with the Cardinals: For infielder Ralph LaPointe and $30,000, the Phillies

enrolled first baseman–outfielder Dick Sisler. The
son of the star first baseman of the 1920s George
Sisler, Dick was a strong left-hand hitter who had
been something of a disappointment with the
Cardinals in 1947, batting just .203 in 46 games.
But the man who two years later would make what
is probably the single most famous swing of the
bat in Phillies history was now on the team.

Also on the team in 1948 was rookie center
fielder Richie Ashburn, a tow-headed, deer-footed
Nebraskan who launched his career with a .333
batting average and league-leading 32 stolen
bases. Ashburn would play twelve years with the
Phillies, winning two batting titles and hitting better than .300 eight times. If he didn't hit many
home runs, neither did he strike out very often.
Frequently among the leaders in hits and walks,
he was an ideal lead-off man. He was also the
National League's top defensive center fielder of
his day. To make this statement about a man who
played contemporaneously with Willie Mays may
sound extravagant, but the statistics support it
conclusively. Ashburn shares (with Max Carey) the

131

Reliever Sylvester ("Blix") Donnelly (1946–1950).

major-league record for most years leading in put-outs by an outfielder (9) and holds the major-league records for most years with 500 or more putouts (4) and most years with 400 or more put-outs (9). An all-time list of the ten top seasons for putouts by major-league outfielders shows Ashburn's name appearing six times. For the length of his career, no outfielder was ever more adept at running down fly balls than Richie Ashburn. (Added to Ashburn's .308 lifetime average, it makes his absence from the Hall of Fame totally unjust.)

Granny Hamner was another new regular on the 1948 Phillies, although playing more second base than shortstop, where the veteran magic-gloved Eddie Miller was posted.

In 1948 the Phillies finished sixth, despite Ashburn's fine rookie season and 30 home runs from Ennis. Harry Walker came down from his stellar 1947 year to .292 and right after the close of the season was traded to the Cubs for power-hitting outfielder Bill Nicholson.

The veterans Dutch Leonard (12–17) and Schoolboy Rowe (10–10) were the only double-figure winners in 1948, although some of the bright stars of the near future were by now working the Shibe Park mound. Roberts was 7–9 for his half year's work. Simmons was 7–13, and at the end of the year the Phillies brought up thirty-one-year-old right-hander Jim Konstanty, who had failed in earlier trials with the Reds and Braves.

Along the way the Phillies had changed managers. Chapman, whose outspokenness had been deflected by his personal relationship with Pennock, finally irritated Carpenter to the point where a change was made. Ben was fired on July 16 and, after coach Dusty Cooke had run the team for eleven games, Carpenter hired Eddie Sawyer, who had been managing the team's Toronto farm club.

Sawyer had been an outfielder in the Yankee farm system in the 1930s and hit well, but never enough to crack the major leagues. He was a highly intelligent, articulate, well-educated man (he was a graduate of Ithaca College, where he taught biology in the off-season). His qualities had been recognized by the Yankees, who employed him as a minor-league manager. Brought into the Phillies organization by Pennock, Eddie was letter-perfect

Eddie Miller (1948–1949), one of the top fielding shortstops of his era.

Granny Hamner (1944–1959), who played second and short for the Phillies.

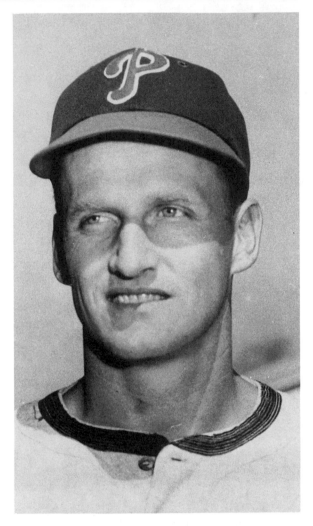

Right-hander Hank Borowy (1949–1950) was
12–12 in 1949.

for his new job. Wise, patient, accessible, and
tough when he had to be, he had an inate gift for
handling men and was particularly skilled at
working with the mix of veterans and youngsters
he found on the Phillies.

Sawyer had managed in the Phillies system for
several years at Utica and then Toronto, so he was
familiar with most of the young players on the
roster. It was Sawyer who had converted Konstanty into a relief pitcher at Toronto, a move that
was soon to write its own chapter of Phillies history.

Behind some suddenly strong pitching, the Phil-

Ken Heintzelman (1947–1952), whose best year
was 17–10 in 1949.

lies took an abrupt leap to third place in 1949, 16 games behind the first-place Dodgers. Pitching it indeed was, because the club batting average of .254 was last in the league, and they were outscored by five other clubs.

Right-hander Russ Meyer, picked up from the Cubs, was 17–8; veteran left-hander Ken Heintzelman was 17–10, the best of his career; Roberts was 15–15, and right-hander Hank Borowy (acquired from the Cubs along with first baseman Eddie Waitkus) was 12–12. Konstanty began displaying his skills as a reliever, appearing in fifty-three games and posting a 9–5 record.

Willie Jones was now at third base, hitting 19 homers, while Seminick hit 24 and Ennis, 25, along with 110 RBIs, most by a Phillies player since Chuck Klein had 120 in 1933.

The 1949 season was marked by one of baseball's most celebrated off-the-field incidents—the near-murder of Eddie Waitkus. The bizarre epi-

Del Ennis.

sode occurred on the night of June 15, while the club was staying at Chicago's Edgewater Beach Hotel. Late that night Waitkus received a note from a young woman in the hotel reading: *It's extremely important that I see you as soon as possible.* A room number was included. His curiosity piqued, Eddie went to the room, knocked, was invited in, opened the door and found the room empty. A moment later a young woman burst out of the closet with a .22-caliber rifle and fired a bullet into the startled Waitkus's chest. The bullet penetrated a lung and lodged near the spine.

Waitkus survived the attack—barely. He was bedridden in a Chicago hospital for several weeks,

First baseman Eddie Waitkus (1949–1953, 1955) survived a near-fatal bullet wound in 1949 to give the Phillies some fine years.

135

part of the time on the critical list. He was, of course, finished for the season but ultimately made a full recovery and went on to resume his career.

His assailant, nineteen-year-old Ruth Ann Steinhagen, was an emotionally disturbed young woman who had developed an obsession for Waitkus when Eddie had played for the Cubs. Perhaps brooding over what she felt was unrequited love, Steinhagen had spun her emotions into an anger that nearly took the life of the hapless Waitkus, a carefree bachelor who had never met the young woman until that night of near-tragedy. She was

subsequently sent to an Illinois mental institution.

The Phillies finished the 1949 season on a note of high excitement, although not for them. With the Dodgers needing a win in the last game of the season to clinch the pennant, the Phillies played them an exciting ten-inning game before finally losing, 9–7. It was the first of three consecutive years in which these two clubs would meet on the last day of the season with a pennant flapping within arm's reach. In 1949 and 1951 the Phillies would merely be part of the supporting cast. But not in 1950.

"We finished sixth in 1948, then third in '49. So while a lot of people may have been surprised when we won the pennant in 1950, that didn't include us. We were an improved club. We were a relaxed, cocky bunch of guys; we knew we could play ball."

The speaker was Robin Roberts, about to launch the half dozen years that would hoist his star among the highest in the baseball galaxy.

A preseason poll taken among the baseball writers found the Phillies the consensual pick for fourth place. But the writers couldn't have known that both Roberts and Simmons were to attain stardom this year, that Konstanty was going to be sterling in relief, and that rookie right-handers Bob Miller and Bubba Church were going to deliver some unexpected victories.

Because of the prominence of so many young players on the squad, the 1950 Philadelphia Phillies were to be labeled "The Whiz Kids" (a takeoff on a popular radio show of the 1940s called "The Quiz Kids," which featured youngsters of astonishing intelligence fielding abstruse questions), one of baseball's memorable team nicknames, along with "Murderer's Row" (the 1927 Yankees) and "The Gashouse Gang" (the 1934 Cardinals).

Roberts, Simmons, Miller, Church, Hamner, Jones, Ennis, Ashburn, and rookie second baseman Mike Goliat were twenty-five years old or younger. The "veterans" included Waitkus, Sisler, and Seminick, none of them older than thirty, and Konstanty, at thirty-three the "old man" of the front-line 1950 Phillies.

The 1950 National League pennant race was an all-Eastern Division show, involving Brooklyn, New York, Boston, and Philadelphia. The Phillies bobbed to the top in May, twice holding first place for a week, fell to third in June, but came on

Six-time 20-game winner Robin Roberts.

strong in July, taking over permanent possession of the top rung on July 25. Behind the strong pitching of Roberts and Simmons and the remarkable relief work of the tireless Konstanty ("He would have pitched every day if I let him," Sawyer said of the palm-balling reliever), and along with solid and timely hitting led by the robust slugging of Ennis, the Phillies built a lead that fluctuated between 5 and 7 games.

Eddie Sawyer, Phillies manager from 1948 to 1952, 1958 to 1959, and for one game in 1960.

Jim Konstanty (1948–1954) was the National League's MVP in 1950.

Emory ("Bubba") Church, who pitched for the Phillies from 1950 to 1952. The right-hander was a 15-game winner in 1951.

Willie ("Puddin' Head") Jones, Phillies third baseman from 1947 to 1959. He hit 25 home runs in 1950.

Right-hander Bob Miller (1949–1958) was 11–6 in 1950, his best year.

Del Ennis.

139

Richie Ashburn. The record book says he was the greatest ball hawk ever to play the outfield.

Through August and into September it looked like an easy wrap. The club began September with a 7-game lead, saw it drop to 4½ a week later, but rebuilt it to 7½ by the fifteenth. On September 20 the lead was still 7½ over Boston, 9 over third-place Brooklyn, with only eleven days to go.

But the first storm cloud had already floated overhead. On September 10 Simmons had left to join his Pennsylvania National Guard unit, suddenly activated as the Korean War, which had erupted two months earlier, began building in intensity.

In rapid order, Sawyer found his pitching staff becoming depleted. Following the departure of Simmons, Miller suffered a back injury and

Church was hit in the face by a line drive off the bat of Cincinnati's Ted Kluszewski. In a few days time, Sawyer had lost three starting pitchers. The Phillies began to totter.

By the time the Phillies arrived in New York for their two final series of the season—one at the Polo Grounds against the Giants, the other at Ebbets Field against the Dodgers—their lead was down to four games, under normal circumstances comfortable, but without regular starting pitching, uneasy.

The Phillies had two doubleheaders in two days at the Polo Grounds and here they suffered a near-fatal disaster, losing all four games. When they arrived in Ebbets Field for their final series of the year, the Phillies had a two-game lead over the host Dodgers with two to play, meaning they couldn't do worse than a tie.

Managed by one-time Phillies skipper Burt Shotton, the Dodgers had been playing spirited baseball over the past two weeks and were now set to consume the wavering Phillies and force a playoff for the pennant.

On Saturday afternoon, the season's penulti-

Second baseman Mike Goliat (1949–1951).

mate day, the Dodgers beat the Phillies, 7–3, moving to one game behind and one to play. On Sunday afternoon the Dodgers sent out their ace, towering right-hander Don Newcombe. Sawyer had little choice.

"It was going to be my fourth start in eight days," Robin Roberts said, "and for some mysterious reason, whether it was youth or enthusiasm or whatever, I had as good stuff on that eighth day as I'd ever had. I should have been worn out, but I wasn't."

Roberts said he couldn't explain why he was able to pitch with such gripping intensity when he "should have been worn out." But a few years later, unwittingly, he did, in a conversation with teammate Gene Conley.

This action took place at Ebbets Field during the next-to-last game of the 1950 season. Andy Seminick is straddling the Dodgers' Duke Snider at home plate, having just tagged Snider out.

Curt Simmons shortly after his National Guard unit was activated in the fall of 1950.

"I asked him one time," Conley said, "Robby, when you've got a runner on third and you need some extra on the ball, do you find yourself pushing off that mound a little harder? He said no, that he pitched the same all the time, that the first pitch goes in as same as the last one. I told him that couldn't be true, because I noticed when there was a man on third and less than two out, that ball popped a little better. 'Well,' he said, 'you can't see what I'm doing. That comes from within.'"

"That was his way of saying it," Conley said. "And I think what he was saying is the very es-

141

Stan Lopata making his momentous putout at home plate of Cal Abrams in the bottom of the ninth inning of the last game of the 1950 season. The play preserved the tie score and set the stage for Dick Sisler's home run in the tenth inning.

sence of the great pitcher, or the great athlete in any difficult situation. He didn't *look* like he was doing anything different, but, boy, he was doing it when he had to."

Pitching against the Dodgers at Ebbets Field on the final day of the 1950 baseball season, Roberts had to do it, and did.

With Newcombe also at top form, the game bore down to the bottom of the ninth inning in a 1–1 tie. Faced with Brooklyn's dynamite-laden lineup, Roberts was just one errant delivery from having his team faced with a pennant playoff and no one to pitch it.

Roberts walked the leadoff man, Cal Abrams. Pee Wee Reese followed with a single to left, Abrams stopping at second. The next batter was Duke Snider, and baseball orthodoxy called for a bunt. Eddie Sawyer, however, wasn't so sure.

"It was far from being a certainty," Sawyer said about the bunt, "because a good many times during the year Snider hadn't bunted in similar situations, particularly against Roberts. Snider liked to hit against Robin. Also, I was trying to think what Burt Shotton was thinking over there on the Dodger bench, and I surmised Burt was

thinking that Roberts might be getting tired and might make a mistake. So I was not sold on the idea that there would be a bunt."

And what was Roberts thinking?

"I thought Snider was going to bunt," he said. "Consequently, I didn't throw the ball hard. I was more intent on getting off the mound and fielding the ball and trying to keep Abrams from getting to third."

Snider swung away and whistled a line drive single into center. Ashburn was on the ball almost instantly, had it as Abrams was turning third and, although not known for a strong arm, fired an accurate one-hopper to catcher Stan Lopata and Abrams was out by 15 feet.

Ashburn was able to make the play because he had been playing shallow. Why, with a long-distance belter like Snider at the plate, had Richie been playing in? According to Roberts, Ashburn had also been anticipating a bunt and wanted to be ready to back up a play at second. According to Sawyer, "Ashburn could play a shallow center field because he had the ability to go back for a ball, particularly in Ebbets Field, where the wall wasn't so far away. And another thing, he knew

Dick Sisler. The man who hit the big home run played for the Phillies from 1948 to 1951. He batted .296 in 1950.

A smiling Dick Sisler is crossing the plate after hitting his memorable home run at Ebbets Field in the top of the tenth inning on the last day of the 1950 season.

that Roberts wasn't going to let Snider hit a ball over his head in a situation like that."

On the play at home, Reese had gone to third and Snider to second. Jackie Robinson, the next batter, was walked, loading the bases. That left Roberts in a still-precarious situation, having to face two extremely dangerous batters, Carl Furillo and Gil Hodges. Summoning those inexplicable resources to which Gene Conley referred, Roberts retired both men, Furillo on a foul pop and Hodges on a fly to Ennis in right.

Robin Roberts: "It wasn't until I walked off the mound after that inning and sat down that I realized how petrified I'd been."

The tension that had settled over Ebbets Field and that had been intensified by the dramatic bottom of the ninth was suddenly shattered in the Phillies' tenth inning. Roberts led off with a single, followed by a Waitkus single. After Ashburn's bunt resulted in a force at third, Dick Sisler stepped to the plate. Sisler's father George had twice batted .400 in his career and collected more than 2,800 hits, but none of them had ever resounded like the one his husky son delivered in the top of the tenth inning of the last game of the 1950 season.

Swinging late on a Newcombe swifty, Sisler lined a hard shot into the lower deck in left field for a 3-run homer. Bingo.

Dick Sisler's teammates come streaming out of the dugout to greet him after his home run. Those are smiles of relief and elation.

The Phillies dressing room was not the most sedate place after the club had won the 1950 pennant at Ebbets Field.

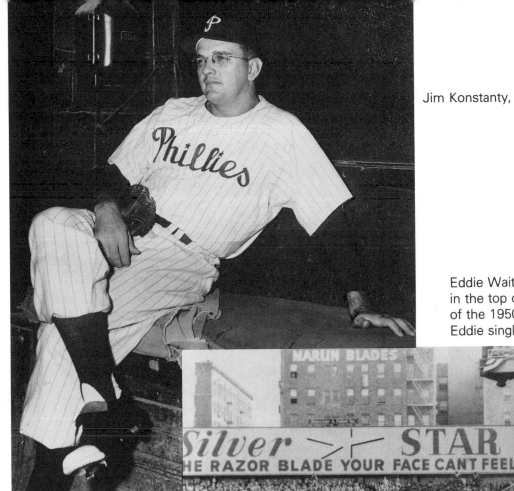

Jim Konstanty, waiting for the call.

Eddie Waitkus facing the Yankees' Eddie Lopat in the top of the first inning of the third game of the 1950 World Series at Yankee Stadium. Eddie singled to right.

Roberts took his 4–1 lead into the bottom of the tenth and retired the Dodgers in order. The Phillies had won their first pennant since 1915—thirty-five years.

With a 91–63 record, the Phillies matched the club high for wins (set by Pat Moran's team in 1916), and their 1,217,035 attendance figure constituted a new franchise high-water mark.

Not only were the Phillies physically and emotionally spent as they headed into the World Series, but they found themselves facing Casey Stengel's New York Yankees, a nonstop juggernaut then in the second of five straight world championship seasons. The Yankees had some first-rate bombardiers in Yogi Berra and veterans Joe DiMaggio and Johnny Mize, along with such

other talents as MVP shortstop Phil Rizzuto and outfielders Hank Bauer and Gene Woodling. But where the Yankees were particularly strong, and in a short series deadly, was on the mound, where they featured Vic Raschi and Allie Reynolds, along with left-handers Eddie Lopat, Tommy Byrne, and, in his rookie year, Whitey Ford.

The Series line score reads: Yankees 4, Phillies 0. But it wasn't really as bad as it sounds. As their predecessors had done in the 1915 Series, the Phillies played it tough and lost it close.

With his starting pitching exhausted, Sawyer gambled and opened the Series at Shibe Park with a man making his first start of the year—Jim Konstanty. The big reliever did an exceptional job, but Raschi was better, limiting the Phillies to two

145

hits in a 1–0 Yankee win. This set the Series pattern. In Game 2 the score went up a single notch on both sides, the Yankees and Reynolds beating Roberts in ten innings on a DiMaggio home run, 2–1.

In Game 3, at Yankee Stadium, the score again went up a notch on each side, the Yankees and Lopat beating Russ Meyer in relief, 3–2, after a strong seven innings by Ken Heintzelman. It all came to an end the following day as Ford, with ninth-inning relief from Reynolds, beat Bob Miller, 5–2.

Philadelphia fans were disappointed but not crushed by their team's World Series defeat. The feeling was that their long-sought pennant had been so closely won that it would have been churlish to expect more. Their club, after all, had hardly been embarrassed by the mighty Yankees, despite the four straight losses.

While the Phillies pitching held up nicely in the Series, limiting the Yankees to a .222 batting average, their own offense had been stifled by the Yankee aces. Only Hamner, with 6 hits, had done much.

As the bright shadows of autumn began to send off to memory the club's most successful season in thirty-five years, Phillies fans could look back on some stellar achievements. Konstanty became the first relief pitcher to win a Most Valuable Player award, thanks to his 16–7 record, 22 saves (saves were not then a recorded statistic and have been computed retroactively), and 74 appearances, at that time a record.

Roberts was 20–11; Simmons, 17–8; and Miller, 11–6. Ennis was the big buster among the hitters, with 31 home runs and a league-leading 126 RBIs, while batting .311. Ashburn batted .303; Sisler, .296; Seminick, .288 (with 24 home runs); Waitkus, .284; Hamner, .270; Jones, .267 (with 25 home runs); and Goliat, .234.

One important factor in the club's success in 1950 was that the regulars stayed healthy throughout the summer, every one of them with the exception of Seminick getting into at least 140 games (a late-season ankle injury helped hold the husky catcher to 130 games).

Although the club's .265 batting average placed them second in the league, their 722 runs were only fourth best. The pitching, however, was tight enough to log a 3.50 ERA, lowest in the league, the first time since the club's previous winner in 1915 that its pitchers had been the league's stingiest.

The Phillies' decline from the heights was immediate: fifth place in 1951. Roberts, still in the early stages of stardom, was 21–15, and Bubba Church was 15–11, but no other pitcher won more than 8 (Simmons was still in military service). Konstantly suffered a complete reversal of form, dropping to 4–11, with only 9 saves.

Among the hitters, Ashburn excelled, batting .344 (second best in the league). Jones and Sisler hit well, but Ennis fell sharply from his big 1950 season, to 15 homers, 73 RBIs, and .267 average.

"It was like a morning-after effect," one writer said of the 1951 club. "They'd had a great year in '50 but just didn't seem to have the energy to crank it up and do it again." The press couldn't resist calling them "The Fizz Kids" or "The Was Kids."

The club played its most exciting game on the last day of the season, when for the third year in a row they were trying to beat the Dodgers out of a pennant. This time, with Brooklyn needing to win to tie the Giants for first place, the game went fourteen innings before Jackie Robinson won it for the Dodgers with a home run. (In the end, all that Jackie's heroics did was set the stage for Bobby Thomson's "Fantasy Island" home run that culminated the Dodger-Giant playoff.)

After the season the Phillies made a card-shuffling trade with the Reds, sending Seminick, Sisler, infielder Eddie Pellagrini and left-hander Niles Jordan to Cincinnati for second baseman Connie Ryan, catcher Smoky Burgess, and right-hander Howie Fox.

With Simmons returning just before the opening of the season, the Phillies were expecting to contend in 1952. But the club got off to a sluggish start, hampered by some clubhouse disharmony that had begun in spring training when Sawyer imposed a set of austere (and unpopular) rules, which included no wives in camp, no golf, no card playing, no swimming. Bubba Church got into the skipper's doghouse and was traded to the Reds for former Phillies outfielder Johnny Wyrostek.

Forrest ("Smoky") Burgess, a catcher with an educated bat. He was with the Phillies from 1952 to early in the 1955 season and averaged .316 during his years in Philadelphia.

Veteran second baseman Connie Ryan, who covered the bag for the Phillies in 1952 and 1953.

Bill Nicholson, onetime National League home-run champion with the Cubs, played for the Phillies from 1949 to 1953.

Shortly after a disastrous 2–10 western trip in June, Sawyer was fired. Carpenter had applied baseball's traditional quick fix to a team's midseason woes—a new manager. So just a year and a half after he had skillfully guided the club to a narrowly won pennant, Sawyer was gone.

Eddie's replacement was a veteran warhorse, Steve O'Neill. A one-time catcher in the American League, the burly O'Neill had managed the Cleveland Indians, Detroit Tigers, and Boston Red Sox, winning a wartime pennant with Detroit in 1945. He had been scouting for the Red Sox when he was hired by Carpenter.

Under the affable, easy-going O'Neill, the Phillies made a sharp U-turn and over the second half of the season were the best team in baseball. After going 28–35 under Sawyer, they played a sharp 59–32 for O'Neill and ended up in fourth place.

Ennis returned to form with 20 homers, 107 RBIs, and a .289 average, while Burgess, Ash-

burn, Waitkus, Wyrostek, and Hamner were between .274 and .289.

Robin Roberts led a pitching staff that scored the league's lowest ERA (3.07). The Phillies ace turned in his pinnacle season with a 28–7 record, most wins in the league since Dizzy Dean's 28 in 1935. Roberts led in innings (330, during which he walked just 45), and complete games (30). If this workload was tiring, Robin didn't show it—he won 21 of his last 23 decisions.

Without benefit of much preseason conditioning, Simmons turned in a 14–8 record and league-high 6 shutouts, Russ Meyer was 13–14, and tall right-hander Karl Drews was 14–15.

O'Neill brought the team home third in 1953, 22 games behind a Dodger club that ran off and hid. Roberts continued racking up innings (347)

Granny Hamner.

Robin Roberts putting in another day at the office.

and victories (23). In turning in 33 complete games in 41 starts, the great right-hander wasn't driven from the mound during a game until July 9, against Brooklyn. Dating back to August 28, 1952, he had completed 28 straight games, including his first 20 starts in 1953.

Simmons was 16–13, after losing a month's pitching time when he cut off the end of his left big toe with his power lawn mower on June 4. Konstanty was 14–10, with O'Neill using the erstwhile relief ace 19 times as a starter.

The offense was led by Ennis and Ashburn, Del hammering 29 homers, driving in 125 runs, and batting .285; Richie batted .330 and lead with 205 hits. So-so as a catcher but always a hitter, Burgess was at .292, although now relinquishing more and more playing time to husky Stan Lopata. Hamner was now playing second base as

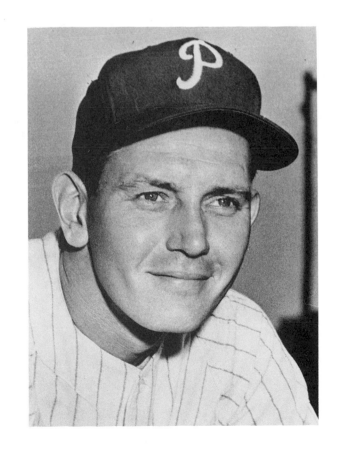

The colorful right-hander Russ Meyer (1949–1952) was 17–8 in 1949.

Karl Drews (1951–1954) posted 14 wins in 1952.

Curt Simmons.

It was July 7, 1953, and Richie Ashburn is holding the ball he struck for his 1,000th major-league hit.

the Phillies tried nineteen-year-old Ted Kazanski at short. It was the beginning of a shortstop-a-year time for the club that would see them playing Kazanski, Bobby Morgan, Roy Smalley, and Hamner again until the position was temporarily stabilized by Chico Fernandez in 1957.

Carpenter hired veteran front-office executive Roy Hamey as general manager in 1954 and inevitably this led to a managerial change. The change, when it did come, seemed ill-conceived:

On July 15, 1954, O'Neill was fired, despite a commendable 40–37 record. Hamey claimed that the team needed more spirited leadership, and the man he chose to provide it was Terry Moore. Moore, in his heyday one of the truly great defensive center fielders with the Cardinals, certainly had played with spirit, but as a manager he was a washout, as Hamey conceded when he fired Moore at the end of the season, citing Terry's "inexperience."

Ted Kazanski, Philadelphia's nineteen-year-old shortstop in 1953; he was with the Phillies from 1953 to 1958.

Steve O'Neill, Phillies manager from 1952 to 1954.

New skipper Terry Moore (right) going over the lineup with coach Earle Combs in July 1954. Both men were stellar center fielders in their playing days, Moore with the Cardinals, Combs with the Yankees.

First baseman Earl Torgeson (1953–1955).

Left to right: Phillies pitchers Karl Drews, Robin Roberts, and Curt Simmons.

Murry Dickson. The well-traveled right-hander was with the Phillies from 1954 to 1956. His 20 losses led the league in 1954.

153

Phillies infielder Bobby Morgan churning up the Ebbets Field real estate in August 1954. Earl Torgeson is welcoming him while Dodgers catcher Roy Campanella is picking up the off-line peg. Morgan was with the Phillies from 1954 to 1957.

The O'Neill-Moore club that ran fourth in 1954 was able to boast Roberts, Ennis, Ashburn, and not too much else. Roberts, the indefatigable ace, was 23–15, again leading in innings (337), complete games (29), and also in strikeouts (185). Ennis hit 25 homers and had 119 RBIs, and Ashburn batted .313, while continuing to haul down fly balls at record pace. In 108 games, Burgess batted .368, but Smoky lacked the at-bats to qualify for the batting race, while the club's other catcher, Lopata, batted .290. Waitkus had been sold to Baltimore in the spring and the club had the veteran Earl Torgeson at first.

Backing up Roberts were Simmons (14–15), former Cincinnati right-hander Herman Wehmeier (10–8), and the veteran Murry Dickson (10–20). In August, Phillies fans felt a note of wistful regret when Konstanty, the relief ace of the 1950 pennant winners, was sold to the Yankees.

There was a significant change in the contours of Philadelphia baseball after the 1954 season. The Athletics were sold and the franchise moved to Kansas City (it was later to relocate further west,

in Oakland). The Phillies, long-time tenants at their home field (the name of which had been changed to Connie Mack Stadium in 1953), soon purchased the ballpark for $1,657,000, and there remained until they moved into Veterans Stadium in 1971.

Terry Moore's successor was Mayo Smith. The forty-year-old Smith, a friendly, sometimes ebullient character, had had a brief playing career as a wartime outfielder with the Athletics, then began managing in the Yankee system, from where Hamey plucked him. Mayo would later go on to manage Cincinnati and Detroit, winning a world championship in 1968 with the latter club. It was Smith's misfortune, however, to be taking over a Phillies team that was to begin an arid spell that by club standards was not long, but when endured one year at a time was long enough.

Headed back to a protracted lodging in last place, the Phillies went gracefully: fourth in 1955, fifth in 1956, fifth again in 1957, before coming to rest on the bottom.

The 1955 club saw its glory come from usual

Robin Roberts warming up in the left-field bullpen at the Polo Grounds.

sources: Roberts was 23–14, again leading in wins, innings (305), and complete games (26); Ashburn won the batting crown with a .338 average; and Ennis hit 29 homers and drove in 120 runs. A 13-game losing streak that started in early May was a sidetracking from which the club never fully recovered, although they did run off an 11-game winning streak in July, which was the longest of any Phillies team of the modern era.

A trade on April 30, 1955 sent Burgess, right-hander Steve Ridzik, and outfielder Stan Palys to the Reds in return for outfielders Glen Gorbous and Jim Greengrass and old friend Andy Seminick. Andy, however, was near the end of the road;

The exterior of Connie Mack Stadium (formerly Shibe Park).

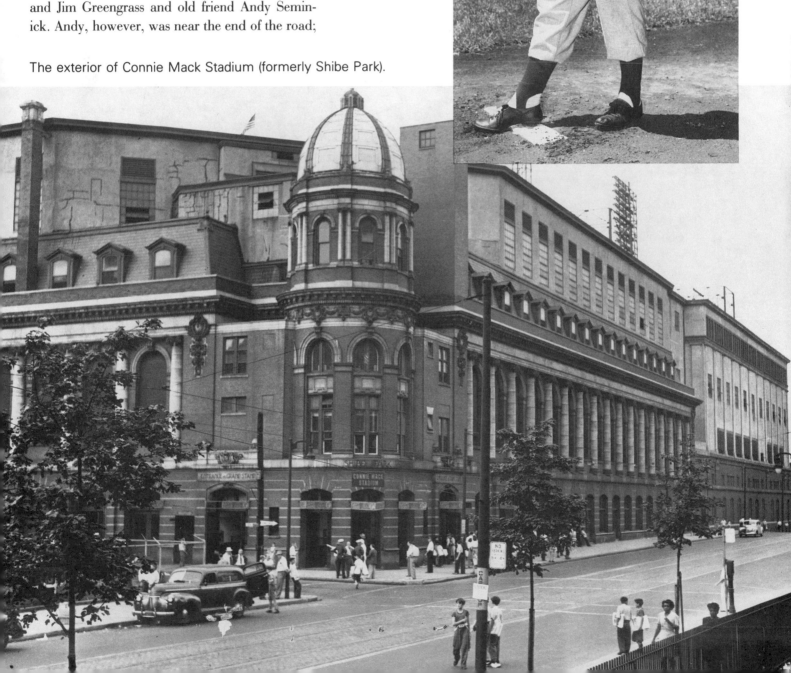

Willie Jones (left) and Robin Roberts celebrating
a victory over the Dodgers at Ebbets Field in
August 1954.

Bob Miller (left) being congratulated by
manager Mayo Smith after a 1956 victory.
Smith managed the Phillies from 1955 to 1958.

Greengrass never hit the long ball in Philadelphia that he did in Cincinnati, and as for Gorbous, his fame would always rest on the fact that on August 1, 1957, while playing for Omaha in the American Association, he threw a baseball 445 feet, 10 inches on the fly, an achievement that earned him a bit of ink in the Guiness Book of Records.

The Whiz Kids, what was left of them now, were a year older in 1956 and, abetted by various pickups from other clubs, finished fifth. After six straight seasons of twenty or more wins, Roberts was 19–18, missing his bid for number twenty on the last day of the season. He would pitch another ten years in the majors, but Robin's twenty-game seasons were behind him now. Simmons was 15–10, his last truly productive year for the Phillies. Saul Rogovin, slowballing reliever Stu Miller, and left-hander Harvey Haddix, all veterans, were new additions to the staff, as was Jack Meyer, a

Steve Ridzik (1950, 1952–1955, 1966), primarily a reliever, was 9–6 in 1953.

hard-throwing righty who gave the club some good innings in relief.

Ashburn batted .303 and Ennis gave the club the last of his star power years with 26 homers and 95 RBIs. Also driving in 95 runs and hitting 32 homers was Lopata, his home-run total a new record for a Phillies right-handed batter, a record that Mike Schmidt would later surpass with regularity.

The 1957 club was to prove competitive for half a season, actually climbing into first place on July 15, but occupied the penthouse for just two days before beginning to slip, with a 9–19 August giving them the big push down to their ultimate fifth-place finish.

The Phillies had traded Ennis to the Cardinals for outfielder Rip Repulski and infielder Bobby

Richie Ashburn on the move.

157

Reserve outfielder Mel Clark (1951–1955)
batted .335 in forty-seven games in 1952.

First baseman Marv Blaylock (1955–1957).

Baseball under the lights at Connie Mack Stadium in 1957.

Left-hander Harvey Haddix (1956–1957) gave the club 12 wins in 1956.

Stan Lopata polishing his shin guards. Stan, who tagged 32 home runs in 1956, caught for the Phillies from 1948 to 1958.

159

Willie Jones.

Morgan (whom the club had previously traded to the Cardinals and who was soon sold to the Cubs). The deal had upset a lot of Philadelphia fans, because Ennis was a local boy and the team's top slugger, but after one good year with the Cardinals Del quickly faded.

In addition to Repulski, other new faces included first baseman Ed Bouchee, shortstop Chico Fernandez, and outfielder Harry Anderson. The biggest impact, however, was made by a couple of freshman pitchers, right-handers Jack Sanford and Dick Farrell, each an extremely hard thrower. Sanford was 19–8, led with 188 strikeouts and was voted the league's Rookie of the Year, the first Phillie to win the award, which had been instituted in 1947. Working strictly in relief, Farrell was 10–2, with 10 saves. For Robin Roberts, it

Jack Meyer (1955–1961), the Phillies' hard-throwing right-handed reliever.

was a season that saw his normal won–lost record go in reverse—10–22.

Bouchee hit 17 home runs and batted .293, second best on the squad to Ashburn's .297. Repulski contributed the top home-run total (20) but drove in only 68 runs, while Anderson parked 17 homers.

The mix of old Phillies and new managed to keep the ship of state buoyant enough for its fifth-place finish in 1957, but a year later the keel cracked and down she went.

The first of four straight wipe-out last-place finishes was in 1958, the first of four progressively worse years that saw the club's losing totals read 85, 90, 95, 107.

The Phillies started off well in 1958, climbing to within 2½ games of first place in early July. By the end of the month, however, they were 8½

Del Ennis zeroing in. Did he hit it?

Humberto ("Chico") Fernandez, Phillies
shortstop from 1957 to 1959.

First baseman Ed Bouchee (1956–1960) batted
.293 in 1957.

Outfielder Harry Anderson (1957–1960) batted
.301 with 23 homers in 1958.

The veteran Jim Hearn (1957–1959) pitched well for the Phillies in relief.

Right-hander Dick Farrell (1956–1961, 1967–1969) after a good workout in spring training. Later a starter for Houston, he was exclusively a reliever for the Phillies.

162

Right-hander Jack Sanford, the Phillies' 19-game–winning Rookie of the Year in 1957.

Even while throwing batting practice in spring training, Robin Roberts was all business.

back and slipping badly—they lost forty-one of their final sixty-nine games and, along the way, their manager. On July 22, 1958, Mayo Smith was out and Eddie Sawyer back in.

"I always had a good personal relationship with Bob Carpenter," Eddie said. "Even after he fired me. We always got along."

So Carpenter had reached for the architect of the club's 1950 glory, but there was little that Sawyer could do but swim with the tide and try not to drown.

What little satisfaction came Philadelphia's way in 1958 came on the final day of the season, when Ashburn put on a crackling under-the-gun perfor-

163

Second baseman Solly Hemus (1956–1958).

Outfielder Dave Philley (1958–1960), one of the most effective pinch hitters in baseball history.

Right-hander Ray Semproch (1958–1959), a 13-game winner in his rookie year.

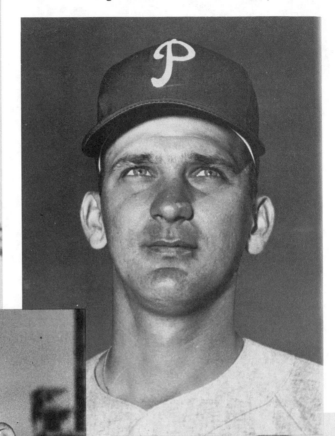

Major-league pitcher and pro basketballer Gene Conley. The tall right-hander was with the Phillies in 1959–1960.

Gene Freese, who played third base for the Phillies in 1959 and hit 23 home runs.

mance, going 3 for 4 to beat out San Francisco's Willie Mays for the batting title, .350 to .347. Along with his second batting title, Ashburn also led with 215 hits and 13 triples.

Harry Anderson hit .301 and led the club with 23 homers and 97 RBIs, figures the big left-handed batter would never approach again. Bouchee, 1957's fine rookie first baseman, missed the first half of the season after being arrested during spring training on a morals charge. After spending several months in treatment he returned and got into eighty-nine games. Solly Hemus, a high-mileage veteran, was at second base that year, batting .284. Another veteran of many ports of call was thirty-eight-year-old Dave Philley, who batted .309 in ninety-one games, doing his most notable work as a pinch hitter. He led the league with 18 pinch hits (in 44 at-bats) and ended the season with eight consecutive pinch knocks, a major-league record (tied by the Mets' Rusty Staub in 1983).

For Robin Roberts it was a year of partial restoration, the veteran working to a 17–14 record.

Second baseman George ("Sparky") Anderson (1959). His future lay elsewhere.

In what proved to be his only successful big-league season, rookie right-hander Ray Semproch was 13–11, while 1957's ace Jack Sanford was 10–13. (After the season, Jack was traded to the Giants for right-hander Ruben Gomez and catcher Valmy Thomas.) Beginning to suffer the arm miseries that would bring his Phillies career to an end, Simmons was 7–14. After a year of virtual inactivity in 1959, he would resurface with the Cardinals and begin a second career as a "canny left-hander," giving the Cards some fine winning seasons.

Baseball is a hard game and last place is last place. Nevertheless, for those fans seeking consolation in disappointment, the Phillies' 69 victories in 1958 tied a record for most games won by a tail ender.

The decade that had begun with a pennant ended with the Phillies in last place, although it was, of course, a team that bore little resemblance to The Whiz Kids. New general manager John Quinn began paring away the club's few remaining connections with 1950's youth-in-bloom team. Hamner was traded to Cleveland in May; and Jones, to the same club a month later. Lopata was dealt to the Braves in a five-man transaction that

Power-hitting outfielder Wally Post (1958–1960) had 22 homers in 1959.

brought right-hander Gene Conley to the Phillies, and after the season one of the brightest careers in Phillies history came to an end when Ashburn was sent to the Cubs.

The club had picked up third baseman Gene Frese (23 homers) and outfielder Wally Post (22 homers), and Bouchee batted .285 with 15 homers; otherwise there wasn't much going on at home plate in 1959 when the Phillies were at bat. The club had bought second baseman George ("Sparky") Anderson from the Dodger farm system, hoping that the twenty-five-year-old hustler would solve the second-base problem. He fielded well, but in his only big-league season as a player, hit just .218.

"I wasn't surprised when George Anderson became a successful big league manager," Sawyer

Don Cardwell (1957–1960).

Right-hander Jim Owens (1955–1956, 1958–1962); 12 wins in 1959 were his best.

said. "In fact, I'd say he was always a manager. He had his head into every game, watching and studying, and always asking intelligent questions."

Roberts, now thirty-two years old, continued to anchor the staff, posting a 15–17 record. Conley was 12–7, and the club got some decent pitching from a quartet of hard-throwing right-handers: Jim Owens (12–12), Don Cardwell (9–10), and relievers Jack Meyer and Dick Farrell. Owens, Meyer, and Farrell were a high-spirited, fun-loving trio who saw no reason why life shouldn't be enjoyed to its fullest. Their exuberant adventures led to writers calling them "The Dalton Gang."

Closing the decade with two straight last-place finishes had Phillies fans wondering if another Dark Age was settling on the team. Well, the coming decade wouldn't be that bad, but it wouldn't be very good either.

ENTER GENE MAUCH

When the Phillies opened the 1960 season, exactly ten years after winning their last pennant, they had one Whiz Kid left and they had the manager of The Whiz Kids. After one game, only the player remained.

Eddie Sawyer had gone through spring training with mixed emotions. A proud, tough man, Eddie realized that his team was heading nowhere and that there was little he could do to help. So after just one game, he did something unprecedented: He resigned. His explanation was tersely to the point: "I'm forty-nine years old and I'd love to

Second baseman Tony Taylor (1960–1971), 1974–1976). His best was .301 in 1970.

Gene Mauch, Phillies manager from 1960 to 1968.

live to be fifty." No manager has ever given a more succinct evaluation of the talent at hand.

To replace Sawyer, the Phillies selected thirty-four-year-old Gene Mauch, then starting the season as manager of the Minneapolis Millers of the American Association. A former big-league infielder of negligible abilities, he had seen service with six different teams. With the Phillies in 1960 he was beginning a big-league managerial career of twenty-six years, during which he ran, in addition to the Phillies, the Montreal Expos, Minnesota Twins, and California Angels. If there was

Right-hander John Buzhardt (1960–1961).

the club: Ashburn had gone to the Cubs for veteran infielder Alvin Dark, right-hander John Buzhardt, and a minor leaguer; Bouchee and Cardwell had also gone to the Cubs, for second baseman Tony Taylor and catcher Cal Neeman; Post and Harry Anderson had been traded to the Reds for outfielders Tony Gonzalez and Lee Walls; Freese had gone to the White Sox for outfielder Johnny Callison. Pancho Herrera was up from the minors to play first base.

The shuffling produced little offensive action. Taylor's .287 topped a team that batted .239, worst in the league and lowest for a Phillies club since 1942. The last Whiz Kid, Robin Roberts, was 12–16, while Farrell, in relief, was 10–6. The club did have a couple of youngsters with live arms in Art Mahaffey (7–3) and lefty Chris Short (6–9), both just twenty-two years old. The club also had another right-hander, a towering twenty-five-year-old named Dallas Green, and while his pitching assured him anonymity, he would be

a consensus during those years of who possessed the keenest managerial mind in baseball it probably would have been Gene Mauch. (Dick Williams once said, "If they ever hold a clinic for managers, Gene Mauch should run it.") Paradoxically, he never won a pennant (he did take two division titles with the Angels in the 1980s). Some people said that Mauch had a tendency to overmanage, that he tried to take complete control of a game that was just too unpredictable for such management. Others maintained that if you stayed close to Mauch you would beat him, a cold-blooded assessment that was sometimes borne out.

In 1960, there was little that Mauch or anyone else could have done with the Phillies, who wandered in last for the third straight year. A series of trades had almost completely changed the face of

Johnny Callison (1960–1969). The hard-hitting outfielder had 31 home runs in 1964 and 32 a year later.

Dallas Green, who pitched
for the Phillies from 1960
to 1964 and again in 1967.
He did better as a manager
later on.

Chris Short (1959–1972), one of the top left-
handers in Phillies history.

Fastballer Art Mahaffey (1960–1965), who won
19 in 1962.

spectacularly heard from in another capacity in the future.

The 1961 Phillies stirred unhappy memories of the wilderness years of the 1930s, losing 107 games, including a major-league record 23 in a row, from July 29 through the first game of a doubleheader on August 20. Despite this hellish season, Mauch felt there was reason for optimism, and the skipper wasn't just reciting the usual managerial rhetoric. Tony Taylor was proving to be an excellent second baseman and the outfield of Gonzalez, Callison, and Dom Demeter (acquired from the Dodgers for Farrell and infielder Joe Koppe) showed real talent (Demeter hit 20 homers in 1961). Mahaffey was 11–19 but awed opposing batters with his fastball—on April 23 he set a club record by fanning 17 Cubs. Short continued to show promise and the club flashed a good reliever in rookie right-hander Jack Baldschun, who led the league with 65 appearances.

Right-hander Cal McLish (1962–1964). He won 13 in 1963.

Right-hander Jack Baldschun (1961–1965), who never appeared in fewer than sixty-five games in each of his five seasons with the Phillies, providing some excellent relief work.

On October 16, 1961, the final Whiz Kid link was severed when the Phillies sold Robin Roberts to the Yankees for a reported $25,000, the size of the bonus the young man had received back in 1947. Hampered by a knee injury, Roberts had labored through a horrendous 1–10 season. The assumption in baseball was that the great pitcher was through—the Yankees certainly thought so, dropping him late in spring training. But Robin came back; signed by the Baltimore Orioles, he gave them three years of winning pitching, then worked for Houston and the Chicago Cubs before retiring in 1966 with a 286–245 record, 234 of his wins coming as a Phillie.

In 1962 the National League expanded to 10 teams, accepting into the fraternity the New York Mets and Houston Colt .45s (later the Astros). This gave the Phillies the opportunity to finish tenth, but they did not take it, instead coming in seventh, a spot that suddenly didn't look as bleak as before. (The two new clubs helped subsidize everyone's well-being with 216 losses.)

Leading the club to its first better than .500 record (81–80) since 1953 was Art Mahaffey, enjoying the biggest year of his career with a 19–14 record. Veteran righty Cal McLish, picked up from the White Sox, was 11–5, Short was 11–9, and Baldschun continued to give the club some of its best relief pitching since the days of Jim Konstanty.

Demeter, playing more third base than outfield in 1962, was the club's top rapper with 29 homers, 107 RBIs, and .307 batting average, while Callison and Gonzalez were each just over .300. Each of these men hit more than 20 homers, as did veteran Roy Sievers (21), who had come from the White Sox in exchange for Buzhardt and infielder Charley Smith.

Roy Sievers, the veteran American League slugger, was with the Phillies from 1962 to 1964.

Don Demeter, who played outfield and third base for the Phillies from 1961 to 1963. In 1962 he hit 29 home runs and batted .307.

The Phillies started off poorly in 1963; in mid-June they were deep in the wilds of the second division, but then began to cohere and suddenly started playing at an impressively efficient pace—56–35 from June 25 to the end of the season. They did this without much help from their ace Mahaffey, whom shoulder and ankle injuries limited to a 7–10 season. Strong-armed rookie right-hander Ray Culp was 14–11 and the veteran McLish, in his last full season, was 13–11. The club continued to get strong relief from Baldschun, backed up that year by the experienced Johnny Klippstein, who pitched for eight big-league teams during his 18-year career. Chris Short, now just across the border from stardom, was 9–12.

Wes Covington, formerly a long baller with the Braves, batted .303 and hit 17 homers; Gonzalez was again better than .300 (.306); Callison hit 26

Right-hander Ray Culp (1963–1966). Twice a 14-game winner for the Phillies, he had his best years later on with the Red Sox.

Johnny Klippstein, who in the course of an 18-year big-league career pitched for eight different teams. In 1963–1964 the right-handed reliever was with the Phillies.

Outfielder Wes Covington (1961–1965) batted .303 in 1963.

one-way shots and batted .284; and Tony Taylor, fast becoming enormously popular in Philadelphia, batted .281. The club now had Bobby Wine at shortstop. Modest of bat, Wine was a snappy fielder with a strong arm. Behind the plate was Clay Dalrymple, who Mauch used in 142 games. In what was to prove the last full year of his fine career, Sievers powered 19 home runs, while Demeter hit 22.

Another veteran who was rounding out his career was third baseman Don Hoak. Ready to take over at third—he played a handful of games at the end of the season—was a twenty-one-year-old power hitter named Richie Allen (called Dick later in his career). Few players ever brought as much bristling talent to the game as Allen. He could hit a ball, as Casey Stengel said, "over buildings." His knockout swings at home plate resulted in piles of strikeouts, but they also produced lots of home runs, RBIs, and a string of .300 batting averages.

Clay Dalrymple (1960–1968), who was the Phillies' regular catcher through most of the 1960s.

Shortstop Bobby Wine (1960, 1962–1968), light of stick but a first-rate fielder.

Despite his superstar talents and notable achievements, Allen's postcareer reputation was to be dominated by the controversies stirred by his stubborn independence. Richie was simply too tough for any manager to handle, but also too gifted to ignore. Rebelling against the obligations that ball players must abide by, Allen would be late for spring training, for batting practice, for games. When he was on the field he hustled and gave every ounce of his formidable talent. Mauch, who was in awe of that talent, tried constantly to talk Allen into focusing on and dedicating himself to the job at hand, but finally admitted failure and for a time was frustrated by what he felt was his own "inadequacy" at convincing Richie that an

173

Veteran third baseman Don Hoak (1963–1964), who finished out his career with the Phillies.

Dick Allen (1963–1969, 1975–1976). Rules were made to be broken.

Connie Mack Stadium in the 1960s.

attitude change was essential. The feeling of inadequacy finally disappeared, Mauch said, "when I realized no one on earth could make him feel that way—except himself. He wants independence. Not family. Not job. Not accomplishments. Only independence. You just can't be that way." Not, Mauch might have added, if you want to participate in team sports. Allen did participate, and successfully, although not as successfully as he could have, his various managers insisted, had he been willing to compromise that fierce independence that remained to the end of paramount importance to him.

Most major-league baseball teams have long histories; the modern era is now nearly a century old. Within that expanse of time many teams have experienced bewildering collapses and excruciating disappointments, some of these due to injuries or inexplicable slumps or the sudden remarkable winning surges of a competitor. The 1938 Pirates, with all preparations already made for a World Series, were stunned by a dramatic late-season defeat to the Cubs and never recovered. The 1951 Brooklyn Dodgers, with a 13½-game lead in mid-August, finished second. The 1978 Boston Red Sox, with a midsummer lead of 14½ games, finished second. Even a club with a relatively short history like the Toronto Blue Jays, in 1987 lost their last seven games and let slip away what had seemed an easy division title.

For the Phillies, the year of black crepe occurred in 1964.

For most of the season, until September 21, in fact, things had gone according to Gene Mauch's plan. Allen was proving to be an explosive hitter (helping to offset the 41 errors he made at third, a position he had never played until he came to the major leagues). Wine and Taylor were at the center of the infield, but first base was weak, with an array of different players being posted there, including John Herrnstein, shortstop Ruben Amaro, Sievers (sold to Washington in midseason)

175

John Boozer (1962–1964, 1966–1969) pitched mostly in relief for the Phillies.

This often happened in Jim Bunning's follow-through. Bunning was with the Phillies from 1964 to 1967 and again in 1970–1971. He was a 19-game winner for three consecutive seasons.

from the West Coast with a 6½-game lead and 12 to play. At that point the standings read

Philadelphia	90–60
St. Louis	83–66
Cincinnati	83–66
San Francisco	83–67

What then transpired was a two-week Phillies disaster. While Mauch's club lost ten straight, the Cardinals won eight in a row, the Reds nine, and the Giants seven of nine.

The Phillies' numbing trip on the toboggan began on September 21 with a 1–0 loss to the Reds, the run coming on a sixth-inning theft of home by Chico Ruiz. Beginning with that game, the Phillies lost three to the Reds and then four to the Braves (including one in 12 innings and another in the top of the ninth). On September 27, after their fourth straight loss to the Braves, the Phillies

Utility infielder Ruben Amaro (1960–1965).

and late-season pickups Frank Thomas and Vic Power. The outfield was Covington, Callison, and Gonzalez; the catcher, Dalrymple.

The club had shored up its starting pitching the previous December by trading Demeter and right-hander Jack Hamilton to the Tigers for ace righty Jim Bunning and catcher Gus Triandos. Bunning filled out a rotation that included Short, Mahaffey, southpaw Dennis Bennett, and Culp, whose season was troubled by a sore arm.

Hovering near the top for most of the season's first half, the Phillies moved into first place on July 16. By August 20, they had built what proved to be the league's largest lead of the year, 7½ games over the Giants (the league was still in a 10-team format).

On September 21 the Phillies returned home

Catcher Gus Triandos (1964–1965).

178

dipped out of first place, never to return. The club then went to St. Louis where they lost three more in a row, the third to a resurrected Curt Simmons (an 18-game winner for the Cardinals that year). After a day off, the Phillies finally broke their losing streak with a 4–3 win over the Reds.

On October 3, the next-to-last day of the season, the Giants lost (eliminating the possibility of a four-way tie), the Cardinals lost, and the Reds and Phillies were idle. The prospects for a three-way tie lay in a Cardinal loss on the final day and a Phillies victory over the Reds, who were tied with the Cardinals. The Cardinals, however, won their game over the Mets, and the Phillies, exacting what bitter satisfaction they could from a season abruptly gone to shreds, beat the Reds out of

a tie with a 10–0 pounding. The final standings read

St. Louis	93–69
Philadelphia	92–70
Cincinnati	92–70
San Francisco	90–72

Neither the Phillies organization nor its fans were in a celebratory mood after their eleventh-hour crumble; nevertheless, there were many high points for the club. Ninety-two victories added up to a new franchise record, as did the 1,425,891 attendance figure.

Among individual achievements were Allen's Rookie of the Year burst to stardom. The twenty-two-year-old power plant generated 29 home runs (a club rookie record), drove in 91 runs, led with 125 runs, had 201 hits, and batted .318. (His year was marred by those 41 errors and by a then-record 138 strikeouts.) Callison ripped 31 homers and drove in 104 runs.

Bunning led the pitchers with a 19–8 record, including a perfect game over the Mets in the opener of a doubleheader at Shea Stadium on June 21, the first National League perfecto of the modern era. (The second game of that double-header saw a 3-hit win by eighteen-year-old right-hander Rick Wise, his first major-league victory. The 3 hits surrendered by the Bunning-Wise combine was the lowest doubleheader total in National League history.) Chris Short was 17–9; Mahaffey, 12–9; and Bennett, 12–14. Pitching well in relief were Baldschun and ex-Dodger right-hander Ed Roebuck.

If there was a critical injury suffered, Phillies fans referred to that of Frank Thomas, who had been acquired from the Mets on August 7. Filling the nagging first base spot for thirty-three games, the veteran was batting .302, with 7 home runs and 26 RBIs. But on September 8 he fractured his thumb sliding. Vic Power, hastily purchased from the California Angels, was unable to pick up the slack.

With the weight of their 1964 debacle on their

Left-hander Dennis Bennett (1962–1964). Won 12 in 1964.

Jim Bunning has just fired a third strike past New York Mets pinch-hitter John Stephenson to complete his perfect game at Shea Stadium on June 21, 1964.

backs, the 1965 Phillies tumbled to sixth place, although setting a record for winning percentage by a sixth-place club in a 10-team league with .528, based on an 85–76 ledger (although once again everyone was helped by the largesse distributed by New York and Houston, who between them passed 209 losses around the league).

The club had themselves a full-time first baseman that year in Dick Stuart, a right-hand–hitting slugger over from the Red Sox in exchange for Dennis Bennett. A big, good-natured extrovert, Stuart batted only .234 but hit 28 homers and drove in 95 runs. He lived to hit home runs, and he had plenty of them in his career (228), but his fielding was so inept that it inspired one of baseball's most creative nicknames, "Dr. Strangeglove."

Allen helped make it a one-two punch with 20 homers, while Callison made it a one-two-three punch with 32 homers and 101 RBIs. Cookie Rojas, who played infield and outfield, batted .303.

The highlights of this comfortable losing season included participation in major-league baseball's first indoor game, the Phillies helping the Houston Astros inaugurate the Astrodome on April 12, 1965 (winning 2–0 on Allen's homer). On May 29, Allen sent a home run soaring over Connie Mack Stadium's left-center field roof that was measured at 529 feet.

The club threw a formidable pair of pitchers at the league all year in Bunning (19–9, 268 strikeouts) and Short (18–11, 237 strikeouts), but with the Dodgers' Sandy Koufax going 26–8 with 382 whiffs, nobody noticed. Nobody noticed either

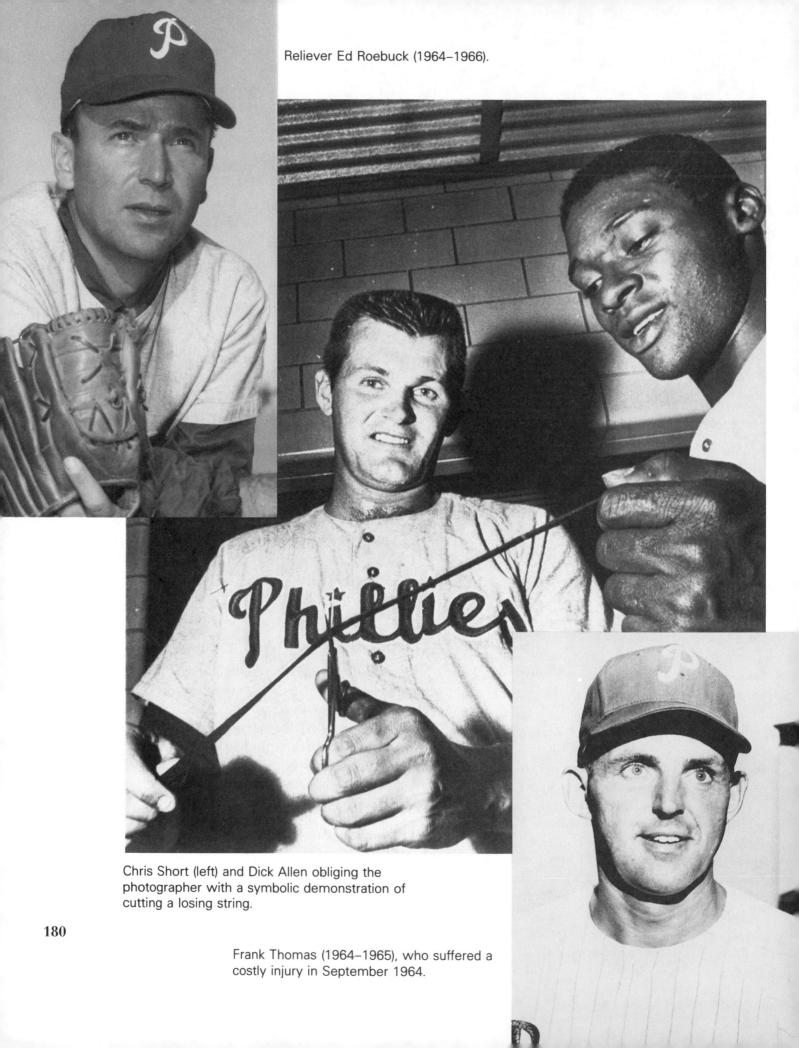

Reliever Ed Roebuck (1964–1966).

Chris Short (left) and Dick Allen obliging the
photographer with a symbolic demonstration of
cutting a losing string.

180

Frank Thomas (1964–1965), who suffered a
costly injury in September 1964.

Octavio ("Cookie") Rojas (1963–1970) played infield and outfield and always gave you your money's worth. He batted .303 in 1965.

when rookie right-hander Ferguson Jenkins made his debut on September 10, working 4⅓ innings of relief in a game that happened to be the club's 10,000th decision since 1900.

The Phillies went into the trade market after the season, swinging a big one with the Cardinals on October 27, 1965. The Phillies sent the moody but talented young outfielder Alex Johnson, Mahaffey (his career just about over), and young catcher Pat Corrales in exchange for first baseman Bill White and shortstop Dick Groat, two fine veterans, and catcher Bob Uecker, who was later to become famous as a quick-witted baseball announcer and television personality. Uecker's big-league career lasted for 6 years with four different

clubs and produced a .200 lifetime average. "It took talent," he said, "to play six years in the big leagues without any talent." (Self-deprecation aside, he was noted as a capable defensive catcher.)

Early in the 1966 season, on April 21, the Phillies traded again, this time with disastrous results. They sent Herrnstein, outfielder Adolfo Phillips,

181

John Briggs, Phillies outfielder from 1964 to 1971. His best was .282 in 1966.

Right-hander Larry Jackson (1966–1968), a 15-game winner in 1966.

(20–10). Jackson made it a Big Three with a 15–13 year, but no one else won more than 7. Left-hander Darold Knowles, who pitched just the one season for the Phillies, headed the bullpen contingent with 69 appearances, logging 13 saves.

The 1967 club kept its head above .500, winning 82 games and coming in fifth. Injuries took their toll: White tore his Achilles tendon in an off-season paddleball game and when he finally got into the lineup in May was never the same player again, the future National League president batting just .250. On August 24, Allen accidentally shoved his hand through the headlight of a car he was pushing and suffered injuries severe enough to end his season.

With a .339 average, Tony Gonzalez finished second in the batting race, and Allen, before his accident, was hitting .307 with 23 homers. Otherwise the hitting was mediocre, with Wine (who returned to shortstop after Groat was sold to the

and twenty-two-year-old Ferguson Jenkins to the Cubs for veteran right-handers Larry Jackson and Bob Buhl.

While neither Herrnstein nor Phillips would weigh heavily in Cubs history, Jenkins was soon to become a perennial twenty-game winner and ultimate Hall-of-Fame entrant. Jackson pitched well for the Phillies for several years, while Buhl logged a 6–8 mark and was gone.

The Phillies were competitive in 1966, winning 87 games and finishing fourth, 8 games out. Allen had a towering year, hitting 40 home runs (his career high), driving in 110 runs, batting .317, and leading in slugging (.632). White backed him up with 22 homers and 103 RBIs, but then there was a power outage, with no one else on the team driving in more than 55 runs.

For the third straight year Bunning was a 19-game winner (19–14), while Short became the first Phillies lefty since Eppa Rixey to win 20

Chris Short.

Giants) batting a near-silent .190 and Dalrymple worse at .172.

Bunning continued his sturdy work, starting 40 games (the most in the league) and running up a 17–15 record, leading with 253 strikeouts and 6 shutouts. (Jim's season could have been much better—he tied an unwanted league record by losing five 1–0 games.) Jackson was 13–15 and Rick Wise, in his first full season, was 11–11. Dick Farrell, who had been reacquired (from the Astros for cash) was 9–6 with 12 saves, working the bullpen with veteran righty Dick Hall, obtained from Baltimore, who was 10–8. Hampered by a knee injury, Short was 9–11.

Outfielder Tony Gonzalez (1960–1968), who topped off at .339 in 1967.

In a deal that was to work out well for them, the Phillies on December 16, 1967, traded Bunning to the Pirates for left-hander Woody Fryman, infielder Don Money, and two minor leaguers. Both Fryman and Money gave the Phillies some capable work, while Bunning's best years were now behind him.

The 1968 Phillies finished in a tie for seventh place and along the way lost their manager. On June 15, with the club playing uninspired ball, Mauch was fired, bringing to an end an 8½-year managerial reign that remains the longest in club history.

The new manager was Bob Skinner, promoted into the job from the Phillies top farm club at San

Bill White (1966–1968), Phillies first baseman and future president of the National League. He had 103 RBIs in 1966.

183

Rick Wise (1964, 1966–1971), an excellent pitcher who gave the Phillies some good seasons, but who will always be best remembered as the man who was traded for Steve Carlton.

At the winter meetings that December, the Phillies purchased first baseman–outfielder Deron Johnson from Atlanta. A strong right-handed hitter whom the club would eventually post at first base, Johnson gave the Phillies several years of respectable power hitting.

On the 100th anniversary of the formation of the first professional baseball team in Cincinnati in 1869, the National League expanded once more, adding stations in Montreal (where Gene Mauch was hired to manage) and San Diego. A 12-team league looked like a fat man on stilts, so the decision was made to break down into two 6-team divisions, East and West, with the winners meeting in a best-of-five (changed in 1985 to best-of-seven) series to decide the pennant winner.

Pennant playoffs, however, were far from the thoughts of Phillies fans in 1969, the first year of divisional play. The team bombed in fifth place with a 63–99 record, kept out of last only by Mauch's Montrealers, who behaved like an expansion club by losing 110 games.

Diego (then still in the Pacific Coast League). The thirty-six-year-old Skinner had had a 12-year career as a National League outfielder, mostly with Pittsburgh, and been regarded as an excellent hitter, four times batting better than .300.

It was "The Year of the Pitcher," and batting averages were down throughout baseball, with the Phillies' no exception. The club batted .233, but three other teams in the league did worse. The best mark among Phillies regulars was Gonzalez's .264, with Allen providing much of the sock with 33 homers and 90 RBIs, the only man on the team to knock in more than 48 runs.

Short was 19–13 in his last big winning season; Jackson, 13–17; and Fryman, 12–14. Jackson, thirty-seven years old and with some quality innings still left in him, retired after the season.

Right-handed reliever Dick Hall (1967–1968).

The Phillies' season was dominated by the hitting and by the antics of Richie Allen. Now a first baseman, Allen hit 32 home runs and drove in 89 runs in 118 games. His game reduction was due in large part to a suspension that lasted from June 24 to July 20.

Allen began haunting Skinner early in May by missing a plane that caused his absence from the lineup for two games. This incurred a $1,000 fine. On June 24 he failed to appear for a twinight-night doubleheader at Shea Stadium and Skinner suspended him. He returned to the lineup on July 24, but then on August 7 he refused to accompany the team to Reading, Pennsylvania, for an exhibition game. Frustrated with what he felt was ownership's appeasement of its star slugger, Skinner resigned that afternoon. His replacement for the remainder of the season was third-base coach George Myatt who, when asked if he thought he could handle Allen, replied, "God Almighty Himself couldn't handle that man."

The club showed some power in this dismal season, hitting 137 home runs, fourth best total in the league. In addition to Allen, five other players homered in double figures: rookie outfielder Larry Hisle (20), Johnson (17), Callison (16), outfielder Johnny Briggs (12), and catcher Mike Ryan (12).

The starting pitching received a severe blow early in the season when Short, after a couple of appearances, was forced to undergo back surgery and missed the rest of the year. Rick Wise emerged as the ace with a 15–13 record, followed by lefty Grant Jackson, a reliever who was pressed into the rotation and responded with a 14–18 record.

At the end of September the Phillies announced the signing of Frank Lucchesi to manage the club. The forty-three-year-old Lucchesi, who never played in the majors, had managed in the minor leagues for nineteen years, fourteen of them in the Phillies system. He was an open, friendly man, a good manager, popular with the fans, and devoted to the organization. His problem was timing: The talent he was handed just wasn't good enough.

Perturbed by the fifth-place finish in 1969 and concerned by an attendance figure (519,414) that was the club's lowest since 1945, Carpenter and GM John Quinn made a couple of postseason

Woody Fryman, a left-hander, worked for the Phillies from 1968 to 1972.

trades. Obviously eager to rid themselves of the "Allen problem," the Phillies barely waited for the end of the season to do it. On October 7 they sent their star player and star headache to the Cardinals along with Cookie Rojas and pitcher Jerry Johnson in exchange for catcher Tim McCarver, left-hander Joe Hoerner, and outfielders Byron Browne and Curt Flood.

The deal became controversial, although Allen had nothing to do with that. Flood refused to report, challenging baseball's right to send him wherever it wanted, challenging, in effect, the re-

185

serve clause. Flood never did report to the Phillies, and while he was taking his fight through the courts (he ultimately lost), the Cardinals sent the Phillies minor-league first baseman Willie Montanez as a replacement.

A month later, the Phillies traded Callison to the Cubs for outfielder Oscar Gamble and right-hander Dick Selma. The club also signed its one-time ace Jim Bunning, who had been released by the Dodgers.

It was a down time in Phillies history, but Carpenter asserted that there was some talent in the farm system and he was correct. Stirring in the minor-league cradles were Greg Luzinski, Bob Boone, Larry Bowa, and shortly farm director Paul Owens would be traveling to Ohio University to scout a young infielder named Mike Schmidt.

Southpaw Grant Jackson (1965–1970) won 14 games in 1969.

The Phillies' 1970 season can probably be summed up by what happened to them on May 2. In that game regular catcher Tim McCarver took a foul tip off the bat of Willie Mays and suffered a broken right hand. Later in the same inning, Willie McCovey slid home into McCarver's replacement Mike Ryan and broke a bone in Ryan's left hand. Lucchesi was forced to shuffle and juggle catchers all season, but with little luck: Mike Compton batted .164; Del Bates, .133; and Scott Reid, .122. Coach Doc Edwards, five years retired (although only thirty-two years old), was also enlisted.

If the injuries of May 2 were an omen, it was a clear one, the club finishing fifth, ½ game out of the cellar. Deron Johnson succeeded Allen at first base and did some Allen-like hitting with 27 homers and 93 RBIs, but second-year-man Larry Hisle struggled to a dismal .205 year, leading the club to give up on this fine hitter a bit prematurely; within a few years Larry would be one of the American League's outstanding hitters with Minnesota and Milwaukee.

The fiery young switch-hitting shortstop Larry Bowa came up that year and there he would remain for a dozen years, one of baseball's surest gloves. By the time of his retirement in 1985, after 2,222 games at the position, Bowa owned the major-league record for highest lifetime fielding average for a shortstop—.980.

One of the signal achievements of Frank Lucchesi's term as Phillies manager was the development of Bowa. After two months into his rookie season, Bowa was unable to lift his average above .200 and omniverous cries were being heard in ever-increasing volume from the stands; but Lucchesi stood firm, saying over and over that "Larry Bowa is my shortstop." By the end of the season

Outfielder–first baseman Deron Johnson (1969–1973) had 34 homers in 1971.

Bowa was a .250 hitter, which was more than enough for a shortstop of his caliber.

The staff leader in 1970 was Rick Wise (13–14), followed by Bunning, who turned in a "last hurrah" season with a 10–15 record. Struggling with a comeback that would never quite succeed, Short was 9–16.

Larry Hisle (1968–1971), who flunked out with the Phillies but later became a slugging star in the American League.

October 1, 1970, marked the end of the baseball season and in Philadelphia the end of another of the grand old ballparks where generations of fans had come to watch their favorite game. Connie Mack Stadium (formerly Shibe Park) was closing after sixty-two years. Like most ballparks built in the dead-ball era, it had an intimacy that its more capacious successors were unable to match, and it had the warmth of created history, a coating that only time could provide.

Veteran's Stadium, which opened for business

Frank Lucchesi, Phillies manager from 1970 to 1972.

on April 10, 1971 (before the then-largest crowd in Pennsylvania baseball history, 55,352), is situated in a complex of sporting facilities that includes the John F. Kennedy Stadium and the Spectrum, the city's largest indoor arena. The dimensions, fairly standard now as new ballparks began opening, are 330 feet down the lines, 370 into the power alleys, and 408 to dead center.

Their new surroundings stimulated Phillies attendance, the club setting a record high in its first year at the Vet with 1,511,233 customers. They were not, however, wholly satisfied customers, as the team belly-whopped into last place with a 67–95 posting, with a 14–30 end-of-the-season tailspin polishing them off.

There were, however, some outstanding individual performances. Rick Wise was 17–14, including a June 23 no-hitter against the Reds, 4–0, in which he became the first no-hit pitcher to hit 2 home runs in his game (he hit 6 for the season). Deron Johnson turned in another solid ner. As the strong-willed Carlton remained adamant in his demands, the Cardinals suddenly acted out of what some people maintained was irritation more than anything else and traded him to the Phillies even-up for Wise.

Wise was a good pitcher and would be for years to come; but Carlton was about to erupt to superstar status. A singular personality, Carlton was to become as well known for his chilly individuality as he was for his lethal slider (baseball's "unhittable pitch"). In an age when media exposure was relentless, he cut off all communication be-

Terry Harmon, who filled in at second, third, and short for the Phillies in 1967 and from 1969 to 1977. He played in just 547 games in ten years.

season of power hitting with 34 home runs and 95 RBIs, and Willie Montanez set a club record for rookies with 30 home runs and drove in 99 runs. Bowa set a league record for fewest errors (11, which he broke with 9 a year later) and a major-league record (since broken) for highest fielding percentage (.987) for a shortstop in 150 games or more.

Rick Wise's fine season proved to have spectacular consequences for the Phillies, and in explanation we must shift to St. Louis. In February 1972 the Cardinals were at an impasse in contract negotiations with left-hander Steve Carlton. In 1970 the tall southpaw had been 10–19, in 1971, 20–9. Faced with a demand for a large increase (Steve was asking for around $75,000, a figure that is quaint by latter-day standards), the Cardinals were wondering which was the real Carlton, the 19-game loser or the 20-game win-

Second baseman Denny Doyle (1970–1973). Notice how far up he's choking that bat.

Mike Ryan, Phillies catcher from 1968 to 1973.

tween himself and the press, print and electronic alike.

Carlton, who maintained a congenial relationship with his teammates (in particular his "personal catcher" Tim McCarver), believed that his aloofness from the press had a reasonable grounding. The big left-hander had been engaging in some new mental and physical disciplines that he believed would aid his concentration on the mound and consequently improve his performances. According to the story that circulated after Carlton had closed the zipper on all interviews, some writers had quoted him out of context on his theories, depicting him, in Carlton's opinion, as woolly headed and pretentious. Thereafter he simply clammed up.

The press may have been irked, but Carlton's silence never bothered the fans. The baseball fan is interested principally in what his heroes do, not what they say, and for Phillies fans Steve Carlton did plenty. In 1972, in fact, he just about did it all.

Carlton's 1972 statistics stand by themselves, without editorial comment: 27–10 won–lost record, 346 innings pitched, 310 strikeouts, 1.97 ERA, 30 complete games, 8 shutouts, a 15-game winning streak, and 22 victories in his last 25 starts. His 27 wins tied the league record for left-handers set by Sandy Koufax in 1966. Carlton became the first Phillies pitcher to win a Cy Young award (the award was instituted in 1956). The vote was unanimous.

It was an extraordinary season under any circumstances, but Carlton's circumstances were these: He was pitching for a team that finished last with a 59–97 record. No other pitcher on the staff won more than 7, and no other starter won more than 4.

Outfielder Oscar Gamble (1970–1972).

Rick Wise at work during his no-hitter against the Reds on June 23, 1971. The batter is George Foster, the catcher Tim McCarver, the umpire Jerry Dale.

Adding further luster to Carlton's season was the fact that the Phillies finished ninth in hitting and eleventh in runs. The club did play superb defense, however, particularly on the left side, where Bowa and third baseman Don Money each led in fielding and each set records. Bowa made the fewest errors ever for a shortstop up to that time (9), and Money set a still-standing record for third basemen by accepting 163 consecutive chances without an error (he also holds the same standard in the American League, established when he was playing for Milwaukee in 1974). With many of Carlton's left-handed deliveries being grounded to the left side, the near-airtight Bowa-Money combine contributed immeasurably to Steve's great success.

The farm system made a substantial contribu-

Southpaw reliever Joe Hoerner (1970–1972, 1975) had a 1.97 ERA in 1971.

Steve Carlton (1972–1986) in 1972, the year he did it all.

Tim McCarver, whose big-league catching career encompassed all or parts of 21 seasons. He was with the Phillies from 1970 to 1972 and again from 1975 to 1980.

Larry Bowa (1970–1981) firing on to first after forcing the Giants' Bill Madlock at second.

One of the slickest fielding of all third basemen, Don Money (1968–1972).

193

Outfielder Bill Robinson (1972–1974, 1982–1983) hit 25 homers in 1973.

tion in outfielder Greg Luzinski, an enormously strong youngster who batted .281 and hit 18 home runs. Two other young men who saw brief action at the end of the season were catcher Bob Boone and third baseman Mike Schmidt. Schmidt got into 13 games and among his 7 hits was his first major-league home run. After that first one, he had 547 left.

While Carlton was winning and the Phillies were losing—which was pretty much the rhythm in 1972—there were changes in the front office and

at the managerial level. On June 3, Paul Owens was promoted from farm director to general manager, succeeding John Quinn, who had occupied the office for 14½ years. Then, on July 10, Lucchesi was let out and it was Owens who replaced him. The GM had no intention of managing beyond the end of the season; being with the team on a daily basis, he said, would enable him to make more intelligent evaluations of his own players and others around the league.

The Phillies had a few postseason announcements. On October 31, 1972, they made a multiplayer swap with the Milwaukee Brewers. To the American League went infielders Don Money and John Vukovich and pitcher Billy Champion, in return for pitchers Jim Lonborg, Ken Brett, Ken Sanders, and Earl Stephenson.

The following day the Phillies named Danny Ozark as manager. Danny was a product of the Dodgers organization, where he had spent thirty-one years as minor-league player, minor-league manager, and big-league coach. Although the press had some good-natured fun with Danny's occasional mangling of the language ("His limitations are limitless," he once said of a rookie outfielder), Ozark was a good baseball man and a skilled handler of younger players.

Shortly after Ozark was hired, there was one more front-office move: Bob Carpenter stepped aside as club president and was replaced by his son, Robert Ruliph Morgan Carpenter III, known to all as "Ruly." At the age of thirty-two, Ruly was the youngest club president in baseball.

The Phillies remained cemented in the cellar in Ozark's first season; nevertheless, progress was clearly evident. The club's 71 victories was a twelve-game improvement over 1972 and the team average jumped 13 points to .249.

The Phillies now had a legitimate seat-smasher in Luzinski (whose formidable physique earned him the nickname "The Bull"), who led the team with 29 homers and 97 RBIs. Another outfielder, Bill Robinson, who had failed in previous trials with the Braves and Yankees, hit 25 homers, and the third outfielder, Del Unser (acquired from Cleveland for Oscar Gamble), batted .289. Settling in behind the plate, Bob Boone caught 145

When he went off to Ohio University "with a T-square and a portfolio," Schmidt said, "I was dead serious about becoming an architect. All I did in my freshman year was stay up nights constructing little models of buildings and doing projects for my art courses."

What he finally ended up building, of course, was a major-league career that earned him acclaim—by many—as the greatest of all third basemen. There was nothing that this sturdy, intense, and highly determined young man could not do on a ball field.

"Because of his power hitting," Dodgers manager Walter Alston said, "you sometimes tend to overlook just how good a fielder Schmidt is. He's quick, sure-handed, strong-armed, he can come

Ruly Carpenter.

Greg Luzinski (1970–1980), one of the genuine big busters in Phillies history.

games, beginning the career that would finally see him catch more games than anyone in big-league history.

Starting pitchers Wayne Twitchell, Brett, Lonborg, and Carlton each won 13, the catch being Carlton's league-high 20 losses. Brett, who could hit (although not nearly as well as younger brother George), set a record for pitchers by homering in four straight games (the only 4 home runs he hit all year).

The most significant addition to the Phillies in 1973 was the stationing at third base of the player who was to become the greatest in the long history of the Philadelphia Phillies: Michael Jack Schmidt.

Outfielder Del Unser (1973–1974, 1979–1982), who delivered a couple of big pinch hits in the 1980 World Series.

in on bunts and throw you out; he can make every play a third baseman has to."

Schmidt got his degree from Ohio University in 1971 and then signed with the Phillies. After a good season in the Pacific Coast League in 1972, the Phillies thought enough of Mike to trade Don Money and open up the third-base bag for Schmidt.

Schmidt's rookie season in 1973 was not auspicious: .196 batting average in 132 games, 18 home runs, 52 RBIs, 136 strikeouts.

"Those statistics didn't mean a damn," Alston said. "All I or anybody else saw when we watched Mike Schmidt was talent, as much talent as you're going to find in a young player."

Right after the 1973 season the Phillies made a good trade, sending Ken Brett to the Pirates for

second baseman Dave Cash, an important step in getting the club out of the cellar. And not only did the club get out of the cellar in 1974, it made a run at the division title for much of the season, holding first place for fifty-one days and as late as August 21 trailing by just 1½ games. A 12–17 September took them out of things, however, and they finished third, 8 games behind.

Many Phillies players said that a June knee injury that removed Luzinski from the lineup for much of the season cost the club the title. But even without the big left-fielder there was solid hitting. Schmidt fulfilled overnight all that had been predicted for him: in a sensational turn-around season, he hit 36 home runs to lead the league, drove in 116 runs, led with a .546 slugging average, and

Right-hander Wayne Twitchell (1971–1977) had five shutouts among his 13 wins in 1973.

Rookie third baseman Mike Schmidt (1972–1989) in 1973.

Philadelphia fans responded to the club's third-place finish by coming out in franchise-record numbers: 1,808,648. It was the first of four consecutive record-setting attendance years.

There were some new faces on the club in 1975 and again the Phillies were a factor in the division race, this time holding a share of the lead until August 18 before slipping back. They finished second to Pittsburgh by 6½ games.

A six-player deal with the Mets brought the Phillies left-handed reliever Tug McGraw, a refreshing, uninhibited, screwballing extrovert. In May 1975 the club traded Montanez to the Giants for Garry Maddox, one of the top defensive center fielders in baseball ("Two-thirds of the earth is covered by water," the saying went, "and the other third is covered by Garry Maddox"). To replace Montanez at first, the club reacquired its

Outfielder–first baseman Willie Montanez (1970–1975, 1982). He hit 30 home runs in 1971. Willie played for nine clubs during his 14-year career.

batted .282. He was the first Phillie to lead in homers since Klein in 1933. Willie Montanez batted .304, and Dave Cash was at .300, rapping 206 hits.

Lonborg led the staff with a 17–13 record, followed by Carlton's 16–13 (plus 240 league-leading strikeouts) and Ron Schueler's 11–16.

Right-hander Ron Schueler (1974–1976), who both started and relieved for the Phillies.

Gene Garber (1974–1978). The Phillies reliever led with 71 appearances in 1975.

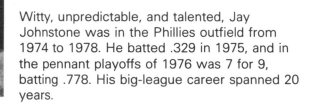

Witty, unpredictable, and talented, Jay Johnstone was in the Phillies outfield from 1974 to 1978. He batted .329 in 1975, and in the pennant playoffs of 1976 was 7 for 9, batting .778. His big-league career spanned 20 years.

onetime premier star and headache Dick Allen. The only trouble Allen gave the team this time around was at the plate—he batted just .233, the power snap gone from his swing (12 home runs).

The second-place Phillies were awash with outstanding performances. Schmidt once again led in home runs (38), but set a team record with 180 strikeouts. Cash and Bowa each batted .305, Cash leading the league with 213 hits. The Philadelphia duo were the first keystone combination since the White Sox's Luke Appling and Cass Michaels in 1949 to each bat .300. Outfielder Jay Johnstone, as zany as they come, batted .329, Maddox .291, and Luzinski .300 with 34 homers and the league's best RBI number, 120. The club's .269 average was third best in the league, its 735 runs second best.

The problem in 1975 was starting pitching. Carlton, still searching for the magic of 1972, was 15–14, while a couple of newcomers, left-hander Tom Underwood and Larry Christenson were 14–13 and 11–6, respectively. Injuries limited Lonborg to 8–6. A bullpen tandem of McGraw and Gene Garber was most effective, with Garber leading in appearances with 71.

The front-office ledgers again inked in a new high in attendance with 1,909,233 tickets sold. The fans were clearly enjoying a resurgent team and expectations for 1976 were high.

Satisfied with their regular lineup, the Phillies opted for additional pitching in the off-season trading market. Accordingly, in December trades they added a couple of veteran arms. From the Cardinals came tall right-hander Ron Reed and from the White Sox lefty Jim Kaat.

"Everybody else is going to pick us to win the division," Ozark said after the deals had been made. "I'll have to go along with them," Danny added, thereby placing himself on the hottest seat a manager can occupy.

VICTORIES AND DISAPPOINTMENTS

A quarter century of losing came to an end for the Phillies in 1976, but under the recently instituted divisional format it had its bittersweet side.

In a season of 162 games' length it may seem rather melodramatic to pick out any single game as pivotal, especially one that took place as early as April 17. Nevertheless, as the 1976 season plowed on through its long schedule, the Phillies game of April 17 seemed more and more to be the foundation on which the team was building its year of success. Playing the Cubs at Wrigley Field on that afternoon, Ozark's men came back from 12–1 and 13–2 deficits to win in ten innings, 18–16. Making the game especially memorable were the 4 home runs delivered by Mike Schmidt, the first not coming until the fifth inning and the last winning it in the tenth. (Mike was the third Phillies player, along with Delahanty and Klein, to homer 4 times in a game.)

From that game on, the Phillies took command, winning 49 of their next 66. They took over first place on May 9 and were never dislodged, but not without first having a scare of monumental proportions, a nightmare that evoked all too chillingly the ghosts of 1964.

On August 25 the Phillies were sitting on a mammoth lead of 15½ games over the Pirates. At that point the pennies began falling on the other side of the fence and the club slipped into an inertia that saw them lose 16 of 21. During this same stretch the Pirates were winning 18 of 22. By September 17 the lead had been cut to 3 games. The Phillies, however, regrouped, won 7 of 9 and on September 26 clinched their first division title with a 4–1 win over Montreal in the first game of a doubleheader. The final margin was 9 games.

Danny Ozark, Phillies manager from 1973 to 1979.

Mike Schmidt, now settled comfortably into superstardom, led the league in home runs (38) for the third year in a row. The Phillies also had an all-.300 outfield in Johnstone (.318), Maddox (.330), and Luzinski (.304, with 21 homers). Overall, the club marked its highest batting average (.272) since 1937.

dance mark was set, this time with 2,480,150 customers.

Unfortunately for the Phillies, their opponent in the pennant playoffs was the team that ranks high on anybody's list of greatest of all time—Cincinnati's "Big Red Machine," managed by former Phillies second baseman Sparky Anderson and featuring a lineup engraved with names like Pete Rose, Johnny Bench, Joe Morgan, Tony Perez, George Foster, Ken Griffey, and Dave Concepcion.

Except for the third game, the Phillies went quietly in their first postseason encounters since 1950. Carlton lost the first game, 6–3, and Lonborg, the second, 6–2. The Phillies took a 6–4 lead into the bottom of the ninth inning of Game 3, but some home-run heroics by Foster and Bench tied it and then the Reds went on to

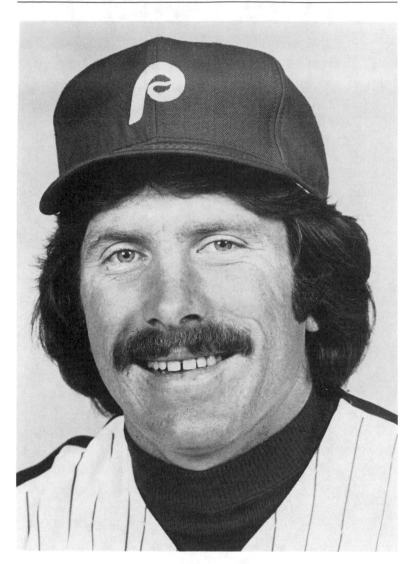

Mike Schmidt, arguably the greatest player in Phillies history.

A benevolent sun shone on Ozark's pitching staff, which was free from injury all season, enabling the skipper to rotate the same five starters right on through the schedule. Starting all but six of the team's games were Carlton (20–7), Lonborg (18–10), Christenson (13–8), Kaat (12–14), and Underwood (10–5). With McGraw, Garber, and Reed on hand, Ozark possessed one of the league's strongest bullpens, the trio notching 36 saves.

With the club winning the division and racking up a franchise record 101 wins, the season was as economically successful as it had been artistic, as for the third year in a row a Philadelphia atten-

Garry Maddox (1975–1986). This superb centerfielder batted .330 in 1976.

It's September 26, 1976, and the Phillies have just clinched their first Eastern Division title. The champagne is flying as Tug McGraw (left) pours it over Mike Schmidt.

score another run and carry off the game and the pennant, 7–6.

The 1977 Phillies ran off the same 101–61 record as the 1976 edition and again it was more than enough for a division title, although this time by only 5 games ahead of a Pirates club that won 96 times.

With Allen gone to free agency (the Phillies had little interest in bringing him back), the club signed free-agent Richie Hebner and posted him at first base, a position he occasionally shared with Tom Hutton and Dave Johnson (the future Mets manager). With Dave Cash signing with Montreal as a free-agent, the Phillies obtained Ted Sizemore from the Dodgers to play second. In a June 15 swap with the Cardinals, the Phillies obtained outfielder Bake McBride in a deal that saw Tom Underwood head west.

After a 1–6 start, the Phillies began to cohere and play consistently winning baseball. They were 18–10 in May; 15–13, in June; 19–11, in July; and then tore the race apart with a 22–7 August that featured the longest winning streak in the club's modern era—13 games. The Phillies, who had been 8½ games behind on June 29, took over first place on August 5 and held the lease for the rest of the season. They clinched the division on September 27 with a noisy 15–9 win over the Cubs.

The Phillies attack was headed by the league's most potent one-two punch, Luzinski and Schmidt. The muscular Luzinski turned in what was to prove his finest season, with 39 home runs, 130 RBIs, and .309 batting average; Schmidt hit 38 homers and drove in 101 runs. It was, in fact, a steady attack up and down the lineup, with Schmidt batting .274 and Hebner, Sizemore, Bowa, Johnstone, and Boone all in the .280s. Af-

Jim Lonborg (1973–1979) gave the Phillies
18 wins in 1976.

204

Jim Kaat (1976–1979), who pitched
in the majors for 25 years.

Left-hander Tom Underwood (1974–1977) won 14 in 1975.

A disconsolate Tom Underwood sitting in the Phillies dugout after surrendering the hit that gave the Reds the win and the pennant in the third and final game of the 1976 pennant playoffs.

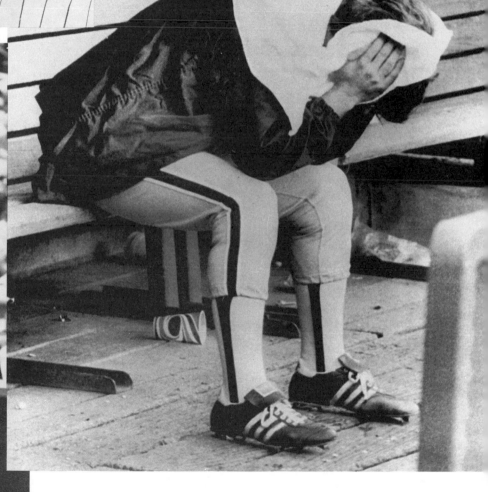

Second baseman Dave Cash (1974–1976) had more than 200 hits in 1974 and again in 1975.

Part-time first baseman and outfielder Tommy Hutton (1972–1977).

Richie Hebner (1977–1978), Phillies first baseman who batted .285 and .283 in his two years with the club.

Outfielder Bake McBride (1977–1981), twice a .300 hitter for the Phillies.

ter joining the club in June, McBride batted .339. The team average of .279 was the best in the league, its 847 runs highest, while 186 home runs set the all-time Phillies record. There are many who believe this was the finest team in franchise history.

Carlton led the pitching with a 23–10 record, a year's work that earned him his second Cy Young award. Larry Christenson had the most regal season of his career at 19–6, Lonborg was 11–4, and left-hander Randy Lerch, 10–6. Once again Ozark had a relief corps that was talented and deep, with McGraw, Garber, Reed, and also righty Warren Brusstar.

Greg Luzinski, who topped off with 39 homers in 1977.

Larry Bowa.

The 1977 National League playoffs saw the Phillies matched with Tom Lasorda's Los Angeles Dodgers. The series was scheduled to open with two games in Los Angeles, and the feeling among Phillies people was that a split in L.A. could very well set the stage for a pennant, because the Phillies had been torrid at Veteran's Stadium (where they had drawn a new record-high 2,700,070 customers), posting a 60–21 mark.

207

Right-hander Larry Christenson (1973–1983), who gave the Phillies an outstanding 19–6 season in 1977.

Catcher Bob Boone (1972–1981), holder of the all-time record for games caught by a major-league catcher.

Warren Brusstar (1977–1982) worked exclusively in relief for the Phillies. The right-hander helped the club to three division titles.

Phillies hopes were buoyed with an opening game victory, 7–5. Ozark's men won it with two in the top of the ninth after Carlton had blown a 5–1 lead in the bottom of the seventh. The Dodgers evened it up the next day, beating Lonborg, 7–1. The series now moved to Veteran's Stadium, with the odds heavily favoring the Phillies.

The third game of the 1977 National League playoffs became one of the all-time Phillies heartbreakers. With the reliable Garber on the mound, the hometown club went into the top of the ninth inning with a 5–3 lead. Garber retired the first two men he faced, giving him eight consecutive ground-ball outs. At this point, a living nightmare began to unfold under the eyes of 63,719 fans.

Pinch hitter Vic Davalillo beat out a bunt. Another pinch hitter, Manny Mota, shot a 2-strike pitch out to deep left field, toward the wall. The ball was catchable; the heavy-legged Luzinski went after it, got his glove on it but could not maintain control of it as he banged into the wall. Davalillo scored and Mota wound up on third with the tying run when the relay was boxed around in the infield.

Even before the next pitch was thrown, the second-guessers were at work, and they had a good case: Why wasn't Jerry Martin in left field? Martin, a more capable defensive player than Luzinski, had often been used as a late-inning replacement for the Bull during the season.

A moment later, things got worse. Davey Lopes rifled a hot smash that caromed off of Schmidt's glove over to an alert Bowa, who picked up the ball and fired to first—in time, so he and the Phillies felt. But umpire Bruce Froemming saw it otherwise and so ruled.

Things continued to unravel for the Phillies. Garber made an errant pick-off throw to first and Lopes moved up a notch. Bill Russell then rapped one on the ground into center field, scoring Lopes with what proved to be the winning run.

The following night, in a game played under atrocious weather conditions, the Dodgers won the pennant with a 4–1 victory. The players and more than 64,000 fans were drenched by an unrelenting rain throughout the evening, but in deference to a nationwide Saturday night television audience, the game was allowed to go on (only the

Outfielder Jerry Martin (1974–1978), who was noted for his defensive play.

most important baseball games are ever played in unplayable conditions). The Dodgers took an early 2-run lead and went on to defeat Carlton, 4–1, and for the second year in a row the Phillies were derailed just short of the World Series depot.

The Phillies took their fans on an emotional roller-coaster ride in the 1978 season, providing thrills and gasps before finally eking out a third straight division title and then once more coming up empty in the playoffs.

The club lost 21 points from their .279 average of the year before, but a June 15 swap engineered by GM Paul Owens turned out to be crucial. On that day Owens acquired right-hander Dick Ruthven from the Braves in exchange for Garber. To replace Garber in the pen, Owens traded Jay Johnstone to the Yankees for reliever Rawley Eastwick. While Eastwick's contribution was min-

imal, Ruthven shored up the rotation with some quality pitching.

In third place at the end of May, the Phillies began the month of June with an 8-game winning streak and continued playing good ball. On June 23 they took a pair of 6–1 victories over the Cubs and with them the division lead, which they never relinquished. By August 12, they held an 11½-game lead over the Pirates. But then Pittsburgh began to sizzle, winning 10 straight, losing 2 and then winning another 11 in a row. The surge cut the Phillies lead to a half game by September 5. At this point the Phillies put together a 6-game win streak, the Pirates began to lose and the lead was built back up to 5 games. Then the Pirates came back to win 6 in a row and when the two Pennsylvania clubs faced each other for a season-closing 4-game series the Phillies held a 3½-game lead. Needing just one win to clinch, Ozark's boys made it theatrical by losing a Friday night doubleheader. But the next day Randy Lerch hit 2 home runs and won a shaky 10–8 game, nailing down the club's third straight division title.

Hampered by a hamstring pull, Schmidt labored through his least-productive season as a regular, just 21 homers and 78 RBIs. His partner in pounding, Luzinski, hit 35 homers and had 101 RBIs. The club's highest average was posted by Bowa (.294), with Maddox, Boone, and Hebner each in the .280s. The team made just 104 errors, lowest for any Phillies outfit in history.

Carlton again led the staff, though this time with 16–13. Ruthven, the key midseason addition, was 13–5; Christenson was 13–14, and Lerch 11–8. McGraw, Reed, and Brusstar were the bullpen stalwarts.

The Phillies remained black-clouded in playoff competition, again losing to the Dodgers in four, the affair capped by one of baseball's inexplicable occurrences—a dropped fly ball by one of the game's master outfielders.

The series opened in Philadelphia with the Dodgers handing the Phillies a couple of thudding body blows—9–5 and 4–0 defeats of Christenson

Dick Ruthven (1973–1975, 1978–1983), a 17-game winner in 1980.

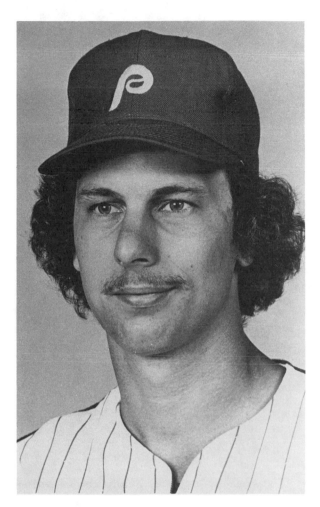

Left-hander Randy Lerch (1975–1980, 1986).

and Lerch. Carlton, for some reason held back until the third game, gave the club a breath of life with a 9–4 win, abetting his pitching with a 3-run homer.

The fourth and final game went to the Dodgers in ten innings, 4–3. With two out and nobody on in the bottom of the tenth, reliever Tug McGraw walked Ron Cey. Dusty Baker followed with a line-drive hit straight out to Maddox in center.

"The ball was right in my glove," a dejected Maddox said later. "It was not a tough play, just a routine line drive."

The ball bounced out of his glove and fell to the grass. Cey stopped at second. A moment later Bill Russell, who had driven in the winning run of game three of the 1977 playoffs, did it again, rapping a single to center, scoring Cey and sending the Dodgers to the World Series and the Phillies, for the third straight year, home.

Steve Carlton; four Cy Young awards.

Frank ("Tug") McGraw (1975–1984), one of the top relievers in Phillies history.

The Phillies were never among the most zealous pursuers of free agents, nevertheless, in December 1978 the club landed one of the most celebrated of them all—Pete Rose. The long-time Cincinnati star had been unable to come to terms with his employers and now was offering his services to the highest bidder. At the age of thirty-seven, Rose was still a prolific line-drive force at home plate, and the Phillies and many other teams were in active pursuit of him, and for a reported $3.2 million they got him, for four years.

The investment in Rose was not misplaced. With the announcement of Rose's signing, advance ticket sales began mounting in startling numbers (the club set a new attendance record in 1979 with 2,775,011 admissions). Nor did Rose disappoint on the field. After having played second, outfield, and third for the Reds, he took over

Ron Reed (1976–1983), who was part of the fine relief corps that helped bring five division titles, two pennants, and a world championship to Philadelphia.

14–12. But two top starters, Ruthven and Christenson, were down for much of the year with injuries.

The game of the year for the Phillies was undoubtedly the one played at Wrigley Field on May 17. Meteorologists didn't have to check their barometers to see which way the wind was blowing that day, they had only to see the score from Wrigley: Phillies 23, Cubs 22, in ten innings. Like the teams' famous 18–16 slugfest of 1976, this one also was won for the Phillies on a tenth-inning Mike Schmidt home run.

The club's indifferent play throughout much of the 1979 season finally cost Danny Ozark his job, the skipper being moved out on August 31. Despite a record of successes, a manager who loses

Pete Rose (1979–1983), a .331 hitter in 1979.

first base for the Phillies, slammed 208 hits and batted .331.

But outside of Rose's fine year and 45 home runs from Schmidt, those throngs of fans had little to cheer about in 1979 as their club, after three straight division titles, finished fourth, 14 games behind. Bowa had his usual near-flawless year in the field, committing just 6 errors in 147 games, teaming with second baseman Manny Trillo to give the Phillies one of the smoothest middle infields seen in a long time, though Trillo, who had come to Philadelphia as part of an eight-man swap with the Cubs, missed fifty games with an injury.

It was injuries that severely damaged the pitching staff in 1979. Carlton, as indestructible as ever, was 18–11, and right-hander Nino Espinosa, acquired from the Mets in exchange for Hebner, was

Mike Schmidt bagging another ground ball.

Steve Carlton (right) and his preferred catcher, Tim McCarver. "They're going to bury us sixty feet, six inches apart," McCarver said.

three consecutive playoff series is standing on ever-thinning ice, and when from out of disappointments rise higher expectations, the manager is almost inevitably doomed.

The new manager, ostensibly on an interim basis, was farm director Dallas Green, who had pitched for the Phillies in the early 1960s. Originally, as Paul Owens had done when he managed

for a few months in 1972, it was Green's intention to manage through the end of the season, get a keener evaluation of the talent and then return to the front office. Dallas, however, did well (19–11), found himself enjoying the excitement and the competition, and was given a contract to manage the club in 1980, which turned out to be the most memorable year in Phillies history.

THE BIG ONE

What made it all the sweeter, when finally it did come, was that the Phillies' first world championship had to be fought and scrambled for, from April through October. The World Series trophy would be the pyramid point of a long season that saw the club win its division by a fingertip margin and then fight their way through the most exciting pennant playoff series in history.

The Phillies began the season sluggishly, playing 6–9 ball in April. The month of May was much better—17–9—and Memorial Day found Green's men in first place. June was a break-even 14–14 month, at the end of which the club was in second place. July wasn't much better, 15–14, and as the season headed into its final third, the Phillies were in third place, 3 games out.

The second weekend in August was, according to some followers of the club, the turning point. The Phillies had just been swept in a 4-game series with the Pirates, casting them further from the top—6 games, in fact. At this point Green exploded, and an explosion from the volatile 6-foot, 5-inch Green was usually worthy of Richter-scale attention. The manager locked the clubhouse door, faced his team and shouted and fumed, searing the air with a fusillade of obscenities that one writer, listening outside in the corridor, later described "as battering the walls like hailstones."

A tirade from so imposing a figure as Green is not easily shrugged off; it generally has impact, sometimes for the better, sometimes not. Some players become offended and remain offended, thus damaging team morale; other players become intimidated and consequently less effective on the field; and still others feel the truths of what the manager is saying—that the team *has* become complacent.

Dallas Green.

Coincidentally or not, the Phillies began playing better ball after receiving Green's verbal bashing. A 6-game winning streak followed, and by August 17 the club was 3½ behind. By the end of the month, during which they were 16–14, the Phillies were just ½ game behind Montreal and Pittsburgh.

On September 1, the Phillies moved into first place, 1 percentage point over their rivals. On September 7, after a 3-game loss to the Dodgers, Green's men returned home in second place, 1

Mike Schmidt; three MVP awards.

at Montreal, the clubs were in a dead heat. The Phillies won the opener, 2–1, and then clinched dramatically the following day, winning in eleven innings on a 2-run homer by Schmidt, capping a 6-game winning streak that carried them to their fourth division title.

Schmidt's blow was most fitting, for it was the crowning shot of a season for which he was the unanimous selection for Most Valuable Player. The Phillies star led the league with 48 home runs (a new record for a third baseman), 121 RBIs, and .624 slugging average.

Schmidt's extraordinary power season dominated the club, for second in homers on the team was Luzinski with 19, followed by Maddox with 11. McBride led the hitters with a .309 average, followed by Trillo's .292, with outfielder Lonnie Smith batting .339 in 100 games. Rose, a .282 hitter this year, led the team with 185 hits and the league with 42 doubles.

For Carlton it was a third Cy Young award, based on a 24–9 record and 286 league-high strikeouts. Ruthven was 17–10 and rookie Bob Walk 11–7. The club received some remarkable down-the-stretch pitching from twenty-one-year-old rookie right-hander Marty Bystrom, who, working under heavy pressure, was 5–0 with a 1.50 ERA in 36 innings. Reed and McGraw again headed the bullpen. McGraw was almost airtight in the second half of the season; after coming off the disabled list on July 19, he was 5–1, with 13 saves and an ERA of 0.52, helping the team win 12 of 16 1-run games after September 1. For the season, the Phillies were 91–71.

Opposing the Phillies in the playoffs were the Houston Astros, winners of their own breathtakingly close division title. After losing their final 3 games of the season to the second-place Dodgers and with it their 3-game lead, the Astros had to beat the surging Dodgers in a 1-game shootout to decide the division title.

The series (still a best-of-five affair) opened in Philadelphia with a 3–1 Carlton-McGraw victory, the big blow a 2-run Luzinski seat buster. For the Phillies, that game turned out to be the "laugher" of the series.

Houston tied it up the next day with a 7–4, ten-inning win. Game 3, in Houston, was a clas-

game out. Five days later a doubleheader loss to the Cardinals put the Phillies 2 games behind Montreal. On September 21, the club had inched back to within ½ game of the Expos. The next day they were ½ game ahead, but on the 23rd they were again ½ game behind. On the 25th they were ½ game ahead, and the following day 1½. But then two losses to Montreal dropped them ½ game out again. By the time the Phillies and Expos squared off for a 3-game season-closing series

Second baseman Manny Trillo (1979–1982)
batted .292 in 1980.

Steve Carlton.

Outfielder Lonnie Smith (1978–1981), who
batted .339 in 1980.

Right-hander Bob Walk (1980), who contributed 11 victories in 1980.

Tug McGraw.

Right-hander Marty Bystrom (1980–1984), who delivered five clutch victories during the 1980 pennant run.

sic. With Christenson and then McGraw opposing knuckleballer Joe Niekro (for ten innings) and then reliever Dave Smith, the game was scoreless going into the bottom of the eleventh, when Houston scored, giving them a 2–1 edge in games.

On the verge of their fourth defeat in four play-off series, the Phillies went into the top of the eighth in Game 4 trailing 2–0, but rallied for 3, only to see the Astros tie it in the bottom of the ninth. In the top of the tenth, hits by Rose, Luzinski, and Trillo scored 2 runs, McGraw held on in the bottom of the inning and the Phillies had a 5–3, series-tying victory.

In Game 5, facing the estimable Nolan Ryan, the Phillies were once more at the coroner's front door in the top of the eighth inning, trailing 5–2, just six outs away from another winter of dejection. But then came one of the great rallies in Phillies history.

Bowa started it with a single. Then Boone hit a ground ball back to Ryan—a notoriously poor fielder—who couldn't handle it. (It was scored a hit.) Greg Gross laid down a perfect bunt and the bases were loaded. Rose worked out a base on balls and the score was 5–3 and Ryan was gone. Lefty Joe Sambito came in and Green pinch-hit Keith Moreland for McBride. Moreland rolled into a force at second, scoring 1 run and leaving men on first and third and one out. It was now 5–4. Righty Ken Forsch came in and fanned Schmidt. But then pinch hitter Del Unser rapped a clutch, game-tying single to right. Trillo then delivered the big blow, a 2-run triple, giving the Phillies a 7–5 lead.

The resolute Astros, however, came back with 2 in the bottom of the eighth to tie it at 7–7. This was the score when the Phillies came to bat in the top of the tenth, making this the fourth extra inning game of the series. Doubles by Unser and Maddox scored what proved to be the game-winning, pennant-winning run, as Ruthven held the Astros in the bottom of the inning.

It was only the club's third pennant in its ninety-seven-year history, and no pennant had ever been more grittily earned.

It might be expected that a club coming off so grinding a pennant race and playoff series would experience some emotional letdown in the World

It's Game 4 of the memorable Philadelphia-Houston playoff series in 1980. Pete Rose is bowling over catcher Bruce Bochy to score the go-ahead run in the top of the tenth inning.

Series, but these Phillies were still high from their recent cliff-hanger escapades and would not be denied. Driven by the relentless Green, steadied by the mighty Schmidt, and spurred by the whooping McGraw, they plunged ahead to bring the franchise its first world championship.

Opposing the Phillies in the 1980 World Series were Jim Frey's Kansas City Royals, whose recent history paralleled the Phillies': three playoff defeats in 1976, 1977, and 1978 and finally a pennant in 1980. The Royals were headed by George

Brett and his .390 batting average, and featured such players as outfielders Willie Wilson and Amos Otis, second baseman Frank White, first baseman Willie Aikens, designated hitter Hal McRae, and pitchers Dennis Leonard, Larry Gura, and ace reliever Dan Quisenberry.

The Series opened in Philadelphia and Game 1 went to the Phillies, 7–6, Walk winning and McGraw saving, the big blow Bake McBride's 3-run homer, which topped off a 5-run third.

Game 2 saw the Phillies again leap out of the fire to rally for four in the bottom of the eighth to take a 6–4 victory, Carlton winning and Reed saving.

In Kansas City now, the Royals took a 4–3, ten-inning thriller, McGraw in relief of Ruthven losing. In this game Schmidt and Brett, the game's premier third basemen, exchanged home runs.

Routing Christenson with a 4-run first inning, the Royals evened the Series in Game 4 by a 5–3 score.

The Phillies' recent pattern of delayed heroics showed again in Game 5. Trailing 3–2 in the top of the ninth, they used a single by Schmidt, pinch-hit double by Unser, and two-out single by Trillo to score 2 runs, then watched McGraw eel out of a bases-loaded cauldron in the bottom of the ninth to seal the 4–3 victory, leaving the Phillies one win shy of their long-sought world championship.

The 1980 baseball season closed down on the night of October 21 at Philadelphia. Behind the reassuring presence on the mound of Steve Carlton, the Phillies built a 4–0 lead after six. When Carlton tired in the top of the eighth the inevitable McGraw took over. Tug retired the Royals at the cost of a run.

McGraw carried the 4–1 lead into the top of the ninth. A walk and two singles loaded the bases with Royals with one out. Frank White then popped a foul in front of the Phillies dugout. Boone raced over, got the ball only to see it pop out of his glove—right into the hands of the ever-alert

An exuberant Ron Reed (center) is being congratulated by coach Ruben Amaro (left) and Tug McGraw after getting the save in Game 2 of the 1980 World Series.

Finally, in 1980, it was the Phillies' turn to celebrate.

Rose. After this crucial, comic opera putout, Mc-Graw struck out Willie Wilson and the whoops and hollers began echoing up and down the Delaware Valley.

It was all summed up, succinctly, emotionally, and definitively by a Phillies fan, who turned to his neighbor and said, "Well, they finally did it."

The question after "finally doing it" was, "Can they do it again?" Well, in 1981 they tried, but nobody really had a fair chance, for this was the strike year, baseball's most bizarre summer, when play was shut down from June 12 to August 10, fully one-third of the schedule.

When play was resumed in August, it was under baseball's most crack-brained design ever—a split season. By the decree of the lords of baseball,

The message on the scoreboard in the rear tells you what Pete Rose (left) and Dallas Green are celebrating.

Outfielder Gary Matthews (1981–1983).

222 Reliever Albert ("Sparky") Lyle (1980–1982) appeared in 899 games during his 16-year career—all in relief.

Utility outfielder Greg Gross (1979–1988). His 143 lifetime pinch hits are third highest total in history.

the winners of each division's severed season would meet in playoffs to determine the divisional winners, then go on to the pennant playoffs, and then to the World Series.

It so happened that Green's Phillies, playing excellent ball before the strike (34–21), were in first place when the walkout began, thus ensuring themselves a spot in the postseason circus. They finished third in the second half, but this had already been made irrelevant; for the first time in history a team was playing the equivalent of half a season with nothing to gain and nothing to lose.

The Phillies lost their shot at a second straight pennant by losing to the division's second-half winners, the Montreal Expos, in five games. Montreal won the first two, the Phillies the next two, but the Expos defeated Carlton in the deciding game, 3–0.

Despite missing one-third of the schedule, Schmidt still hit 31 homers (giving him his fifth home run title), led in RBIs for the second straight year with 91 (in 102 games), and was voted his second straight MVP award. Given a full schedule in 1981, Mike, who batted .316, might well have had his greatest year ever.

Rose led in hits with 140 and batted .325, while newcomer Gary Matthews batted .301. With Luzinski having been sold to the White Sox, the Phillies needed a new left-fielder and Matthews was the man they obtained, getting him from the Braves for pitcher Bob Walk. It was a good trade for the Phillies, for Matthews brought to the ballpark with him not only talent but an engaging personality and winning, upbeat attitude.

Carlton was superb in the abbreviated season, posting a 13–4 record, and Ruthven was 12–7.

Getting into a handful of games at the end of the season was twenty-one-year-old infielder Ryne Sandberg, taking the first tentative steps of what was to be a scintillating career. Unfortunately for the partisans at Veterans Stadium, that career would unfold in Wrigley Field.

When Dallas Green decided to leave the Phillies to become general manager of the Cubs, the team lost more than a manager. One of Green's first moves as Cubs GM was to make a swap with his former employers. To the Phillies went shortstop Ivan DeJesus in exchange for Bowa and a minor-league "throw-in," Ryne Sandberg. (Green was later to finesse the Phillies out of Keith Moreland, Dick Ruthven, Gary Matthews, and Bob Dernier, all of whom helped the Cubs to a division title in 1984. The Phillies had little of value to show for these transactions.)

In the fall of 1981, after nearly forty years in Philadelphia baseball, the Carpenter family decided to sell out. Reportedly, Ruly Carpenter was alarmed and exasperated by what appeared to be the irrational escalations of salaries. His decision to get out underlined baseball's peculiar corporate structure, whereby twenty-six teams are at the same time partners and competitors; where on the one hand there is a vested interest in keeping costs and salaries down, there is on the other a commitment and an obligation to winning, which most owners feel can be accomplished only by further and larger expenditures on playing talent, a situation that free agency exacerbated and Ruly Carpenter could no longer tolerate.

Ryne Sandberg (1981). He had just six at bats in a Phillies uniform.

edge of the complexities of operating a major-league team (although Giles was known to smile wryly and concede that the Phillies had been "skinned" in some of their swaps with Dallas Green).

Taking over as manager in 1982 was Pat Corrales, who had been a backup catcher with the club in the 1960s. The rugged but soft-spoken Corrales guided his new team through what turned out to be a season of frustration and lost opportunities. The club got off poorly in April, bumbling to a 6–13 record, turned it around with a 19–8 May and settled into the pennant race.

The Phillies were in first place, either sharing or alone, from July 11 through August 12 and as late as September 13. After that, well, Corrales summed up the season when he said, "When I look back on 1982 I'll always remember our horrible start and the last three weeks." A dry spell

Heading the group that bought the team for a reported $30 million was as pure-blooded a base-ball executive as one might find—Bill Giles. The son of former Cincinnati Reds GM and National League president Warren Giles, young Bill had gone to work as a summer employee of the Reds while he was still in college. After graduation, he began carving out his career on a full-time basis, first with the Reds and then with Houston. In 1969, he joined the Phillies as vice-president of business operations, working his way up to executive vice-president. A versatile front-office man, Giles had won respect not only for his business acumen but also for his general all-around knowl-

224

Shortstop Ivan DeJesus (1982–1984).

Bill Giles.

Pat Corrales, catcher with the Phillies in 1964
and 1965, and manager in 1982 and 1983.

Pete Rose scoring the Pete Rose way.

of four wins in thirteen games combined with an eight-game Cardinal winning streak was enough to drop the Phillies into second place at the end, just three games short of the top.

For Steve Carlton it was another year of high personal achievement. The major leagues' only twenty-game winner (23–11), he led in strikeouts (286), shutouts (6), and complete games (19), and the baseball writers, with whom he continued to maintain his sphinxlike pose, voted him an unprecedented fourth Cy Young award. Right-hander Mike Krukow, who had come from the Cubs in the Keith Moreland deal, was 13–11 (Mike was traded to the Giants after the season for second baseman Joe Morgan and lefty reliever Al Holland). Dick Ruthven was 11–11 (he would be swapped to the Cubs the following spring).

Schmidt remained the core of the attack, hitting 35 home runs, but with some light hitting around him drove in just 87 runs. Maddox and Matthews were in the .280s. With long-time catcher Bob Boone having been sold to the California Angels, the Phils had Bo Diaz behind the plate. Bo had a strong arm and, in 1982, a pretty strong bat, hitting 18 home runs and compiling a .288 average.

For Manny Trillo it was a year for the record books. The Phillies second baseman set major-league standards for second basemen with 89 consecutive errorless games in a season (broken by Sandberg in 1989) and 479 consecutive errorless chances.

When Trillo asked for a long-term contract after the season he found himself on the way to Cleveland. In what was rather an eye-catching transaction, the Phillies traded Trillo, outfielder George Vukovich, shortstop Julio Franco, and two minor leaguers for outfielder Von Hayes. The five-

Joe Morgan played 22 years in the big leagues, one of them (1983) with the Phillies.

Hard-throwing left-handed reliever Al Holland (1983–1985) had 29 saves in 1984.

Catcher Beaudilio ("Bo") Diaz (1982–1985) had 18 homers in 1982.

for-one deal automatically put Hayes under a lot of pressure. The twenty-four-year-old had batted .250 for Cleveland in 1982, with 14 home runs. Despite those modest numbers, the Phillies organization believed the rangy, 6-foot, 5-inch outfielder was a fountain of untapped talent.

The first Phillies pennant was twenty-eight years in the coming, the second was a thirty-five year wait and the third took thirty years. But Phillies fans who were prepared to Rip-Van-Winkle-it while waiting for the next pennant were pleasantly surprised in 1983.

This was the Phillies club that included three veteran onetime cogs of Cincinnati's "Big Red Machine," with Pete Rose at first base, Joe Morgan at second, and Tony Perez pinch-hitting and spelling Rose. With the mileage on these three and some of the other Phillies stalwarts, some press

box wags couldn't resist calling the team "The Wheeze Kids."

It was a strange, hybrid crew, but they played just well enough to win, and for a group of alleged graybeards they won it in rather surprising fashion—with a terrific September surge. Tied with the Pirates for the lead on September 15, the Phillies suddenly tore off an 11-game winning streak that rode them to their fifth division title, won by a final margin of 6 games over the Pirates.

Outside of Schmidt's league-leading 40 home runs, there wasn't any notable hitting among the division winners. Rose, who was released after the season, batted just .245; Hayes, .265; Maddox, .275; Matthews, .258, Diaz, .236; DeJesus, .254; and Morgan, .230. The secret ingredient was timeliness. Despite a .249 batting average that was ninth best in the league, the club scored 696 runs, which ranked third. Morgan, in particular, did some hard hitting down the stretch, and Phillies

Von Hayes, who joined the Phillies in 1983. The club traded five players to get him.

players were quick to point out that some heavy hitting by Perez during the early part of the season had helped win a lot of games for the team.

The Phillies pitching staff delivered another Cy Young award winner that year, but this time it wasn't Steve Carlton, but rather right-hander John Denny, who had been picked up from Cleveland late in the 1982 season. Putting together the year of his life, Denny was 19–6. The only other starter to win in double figures was Carlton, whose 15–16 record included his 300th career win on September 23. With the starting pitching so ragged, the calls to the bullpen were frequent and the responses sterling. The club had three pitchers appearing in more than 60 games each: Reed, who was 9–1 with 8 saves; lefty Willie Hernandez (picked up from the Cubs), who was 8–4 with 7 saves; and the closer, Al Holland, who was 8–4 with 25 saves.

Along the way, manager Pat Corrales had a

Phillies front-office executive Paul Owens, who also managed the club in 1972 and 1983–1984, winning the pennant in 1983.

Right-hander John Denny (1982–1985), who won 19 games and a Cy Young award in 1983.

unique experience: He was fired with his club in first place. Eighty-five games into the season, with the team sporting a 43–42 record and resting narrowly in first place, Paul Owens decided that Pat wasn't getting the most out of the talent at hand and, as he had done in 1972, came down from the front office and picked up the reins himself. "The Pope," as he was known within Phillies circles, then went on to prove his point, leading the club to a 47–30 finish and the title.

This time the playoff series held no traumas and very little drama for the Phillies, who were matched with their former playoff tormentors, the Los Angeles Dodgers. In the opener, at LA, Carlton and Holland teamed to eke out a 1–0 victory, the run scoring on Schmidt's first-inning homer. After the Dodgers came back to beat Denny the next day, 4–1, the series moved to Philadelphia and a couple of easy hometown victories.

In Game 3, rookie right-hander Charlie Hud-

Mike Schmidt didn't always get them, but he always tried. This action is from the 1983 World Series.

son, an early season call-up from the minors, went all the way in a 7–2 win. The Phillies nailed the flag to the mast the next day as Carlton, with late-inning assistance from Reed and Holland, won by the same 7–2 score. The hitting star of the four-game set was Gary Matthews, with 3 home runs and 8 runs batted in.

The 1983 World Series was a neighborly affair—Philadelphia versus Baltimore. Joe Altobelli's club had the American League MVP in young shortstop Cal Ripken and a bona fide socker in first baseman Eddie Murray, plus a cast of platoon players that Altobelli had manipulated masterfully throughout the season. The O's also had a phalanx of good starters in Mike Boddicker, Storm Davis, and lefties Mike Flanagan and Scott McGregor, and a pair of tough relievers in Sammy Stewart and left-hander Tippy Martinez.

High tide for the Phillies in the 1983 Series came early and immediately subsided. With Holland nailing down the final four outs for Denny, the Phillies won the opener at Baltimore, 2–1, scoring on home runs by Morgan and Maddox.

After that, it was strictly an Oriole show.

Baltimore took Game 2, beating Hudson, 4–1. In Philadelphia, the O's edged out a 3–2 win in Game 3, beating Carlton. Game 4 was also close, the Orioles winning it 5–4, beating Denny. It was all over the following night as McGregor glided to a 5–0 trimming of Hudson.

For Mike Schmidt the Series was a nightmare—1 hit in twenty tries for an .050 batting average. But his mates didn't light any fires either, batting just .195 over the five-game affair.

The 1984 Phillies finished fourth with a break-even 81–81 record, but it might have been better. The club led the league with a .266 batting average and 147 home runs and were second with 720 runs. But a leaky defense that committed 161 errors and turned the league's fewest double plays (112) and allowed the most unearned runs (104) helped to founder the ship. A glut of injuries also hurt.

As ever, Mike Schmidt hit the long ball, tying for the lead in home runs (36) and RBIs (106). Rookie second baseman Juan Samuel hit well,

Bystrom, was 10–6. The Phillies bullpen, its strength in 1983, was further depleted (after trading Reed) by a spring trade that saw Willie Hernandez go to the Tigers for outfielder Glenn Wilson. This deal proved to be a glare in the eyes of the Phillies all season as Willie's spectacular relief work in Detroit earned him both Cy Young and MVP honors as he helped pitch his club to a world championship. Overworked in the pen, Holland, after a good start, faded in the second half.

Adding to the Phillies' discomfort in the 1984 season (which closed with a 9-game losing streak) was watching a group of ex-Phillie players help the Cubs to the division title. The expatriates included Ryne Sandberg (the league's MVP), Larry Bowa, Bob Dernier, Keith Moreland, Gary Matthews, and Dick Ruthven.

Second baseman Juan Samuel (1983–1989). His 19 triples in 1984 are the all-time Phillies club record.

Veteran left-hander Jerry Koosman (1984–1985), who wound up his 19-year career with the Phillies.

batting .272, collecting 191 hits, among them a club record 19 triples and set another club record with 72 stolen bases. But Juan also had his drawbacks, namely a league-high 168 strikeouts and 33 errors. Hayes began paying off on the five-for-one deal with a .292 average and 48 stolen bases.

With Rose gone, Len Matuszek was at first, but injuries limited him to 262 at bats. Injuries also impeded Maddox, Diaz, and Denny, who dropped from 19–6 to 7–7. In his final productive year, Carlton was 13–7, while forty-one-year-old lefty Jerry Koosman, acquired from the White Sox in exchange for Reed, was 14–15. Another lefty newcomer, Shane Rawley, obtained in a June 30 swap with the Yankees for onetime flash Marty

Kevin Gross (1983–1988) won 15 in 1985.

gust were unable to firm up. An 11-game September-October losing streak provided a fitting coda to an empty season that saw the club finish fifth. There was, however, one thunderous out-burst that helped rewrite the club record book. On June 11, with the New York Mets the hapless victims, the Phillies ran up a 26–7 victory, getting 27 hits, both the run and hit totals new highs for the franchise. Von Hayes homered twice in the bottom of a 9-run first inning, the second shot a grand slam (oddly, the only home runs of the game). The Phillies scored seven more in the bot-tom of the second, making it 16–0 at that point. Among the mayhem were 10 Phillies doubles, which set another club record for one game.

A strained rotator cuff sidelined Carlton for three months and left him with a 1–8 record and his career down to its sediment. An ailing knee

Kent Tekulve, the long-time Pirate bullpen ace, worked for the Phillies from 1985 to 1988.

Paul Owens returned to the front office after the 1984 season and the new skipper was John Felske. The forty-three-year-old Felske had spent most of his playing career as a minor-league catcher, with brief trials with the Cubs and Brew-ers. He had put in eight years as a minor-league manager and the 1984 season as a coach with the Phillies.

Felske's big-league managerial career started on a down note, the club opening the 1985 season by losing 8 of its first 9 games, a beginning that sounded a keynote for the coming months. An 8–11 April and 9–17 May turned the footing to a quicksand that winning records in June and Au-

232

Third baseman Rick Schu (1984–1987).

1986, but hardly caused any excitement, for if there was a race in the National League East that year it was by the New York Mets to see how many games they could win (they ended up with 108). Cardinals manager Whitey Herzog announced—startlingly but accurately—in June that the race was over. New York's bulge over Philadelphia was 21½.

The season saw Schmidt return to third base, where he settled in to hit 37 homers, lead for a league-record eighth time, lead with 119 RBIs, and won his third MVP award. Hayes was moved to

finished Koosman, who bowed out with a 6–4 record. Right-hander Kevin Gross was 15–13, leading the staff, with Rawley checking in at 13–8. Submarine-balling right-hander Kent Tekulve, long the mainstay of the Pittsburgh bullpen, came in a trade for Al Holland and saved 14 games.

Hoping to break Rick Schu in at third, the club switched Schmidt to first base where he played 106 games and adapted well. Now thirty-five years old, the future Hall of Famer remained the heart and soul of the club's attack, slamming 33 homers and driving in 93 runs. The top RBI man, however, was Glenn Wilson with 102. Catcher Ozzie Virgil hit 19 homers, and after the season was traded to the Braves for outfielder Milt Thompson and the man the Phillies wanted to stabilize their bullpen, fastballing right-hander Steve Bedrosian. Samuel cut his errors to 15, stole 53 bases, but continued to be bedeviled by strikeouts, amassing a league high 141.

Felske moved the club up to second place in

Glenn Wilson (1984–1987). The strong-armed outfielder had 102 RBIs in 1985.

Catcher Ozzie Virgil (1980–1985) had 19 homers in 1985.

Outfielder Milt Thompson (1986–1988) batted .302 in 1987.

Mike Schmidt.

Don Carman, who joined the Phillies in 1983.
He won 13 in 1987.

first base and there gave the club an excellent season, batting .305, knocking in 98 runs and leading the league in doubles (46) and runs (107).

On June 24 the Phillies released Steve Carlton, who had been struggling with a 4–8 record and 6.18 ERA. At the age of forty-one, the man who had been the league's dominant southpaw for more than a decade, was just about finished, though he stubbornly held on for another three years, pitching for four different teams, with little success. Carlton pitched for the Phillies for fifteen years, longer than any other man in club history, leaving behind an array of team records, including most victories (241) and most strikeouts (3,031).

The departure of Carlton and an injury to Rawley opened the starting rotation to left-handers Don Carman (10–5) and Bruce Ruffin (9–4), Carman being hauled in from the bullpen. At 12–12, Gross

Bruce Ruffin was 9–4 in 1986, his rookie year.

The Phillies were 29–32 on June 18 when Felske was fired and replaced by Lee Elia, formerly manager of the Cubs. The change made little difference, Elia running up a 51–50 record and ending in a fourth-place tie. The team got to within 6½ of first place as late as August 22, but then dropped 25 of its last 39.

The bullpen produced the league's Cy Young award winner in 1987 in Bedrosian, who set a new club record with 40 saves. The fastballing righty was helped by some remarkable work from

Lance Parrish (1987–1988). Two disappointing years in Philadelphia.

was the team's top winner in 1986. The bullpen was well served that year, with Tekulve getting into seventy-three games and setting things up for Steve Bedrosian, who tied the club record with 29 saves.

The Phillies were guilty of an oversight that year. They had right-hander Dave Stewart on the staff at the opening of the season, worked him a few times and then early in May released him. He was subsequently picked up by the Oakland Athletics, for whom he soon began reeling off a series of strong-armed twenty-game victory seasons.

Felske and his squad were feeling upbeat as the 1987 campaign opened, thanks primarily to the signing of free-agent catcher Lance Parrish, for years one of the game's best receivers with the Detroit Tigers. Parrish's problems, however, reflected the club's as a whole. The power-hitting catcher batted .188 in April and by the end of May had just 4 home runs.

John Felske (right), Phillies manager from 1985 to 1987. The other man is coach Lee Elia, who would be Felske's successor.

Lee Elia, Phillies manager in 1987–1988.

Right-hander Steve Bedrosian, who had 40 saves and a Cy Young award in 1987. He was with the Phillies from 1986 to 1989.

Shane Rawley (1984–1988) won 17 in 1987.

his bullpen partner Tekulve; the forty-year-old reliever worked in ninety games, most ever by a Phillies pitcher. Rawley was the ace at 17–11 but was winless in his last 7 starts, costing him a shot at Cy Young honors. Carman was 13–11 and Ruffin, 11–14, while Gross, set off track by a back problem in the spring, slumped to 9–16.

Parrish never did hit with the authority he had shown in Detroit, ending the season with 17 homers and a .245 batting average. Schmidt was again the top gun, hitting 35 homers and driving in 113 runs and Hayes punched 21 one-way tickets. Among Schmidt's homers was his 500th career shot, hit on April 18, making him only the fourteenth player to reach that plateau. Samuel continued to be an offensive force, hitting 28 homers, 15 triples, and 37 doubles; driving in 100 runs; and stealing 35 bases. He became the first player to record double figures in homers, triples, doubles, and stolen bases in each of his first four years. The second baseman continued to undercut his value, however, by leading in strikeouts for the fourth straight year with 162.

Outfielder Milt Thompson gave the club a year of unexpected quality in 1987 with a .302 average and 42 stolen bases, and outfielder Chris James, brought up from the club's Maine farm team after the start of the season, batted .293. Glenn Wilson's RBIs and batting average had been decreasing each year, but the cannon-armed right-fielder's throwing never faltered as he led league outfielders in assists for the third straight year with 18. But after a December 1987 trade with Seattle that brought outfielder Phil Bradley to Philadelphia, Wilson headed to the American League.

The Phillies were now stuck in a mode of "get worse before get better," and worse duly arrived in 1988 with a thudding last place finish with a record of 65–96. It was their first dust-bin terminus since 1973.

The 1988 team endured slumps, off-seasons, and injuries. Even the hitherto indestructible Schmidt was affected. After a sluggish first half, he went out on August 13 with a torn rotator cuff and ended the season with just 12 home runs and a .249 average. The thirty-eight-year-old star promised a comeback in 1989, but the shadows around him were extremely long. Parrish never

Mike Schmidt, Philadelphia's 8-time home-run champ.

did hit in Philadelphia, dropping to 15 homers and a .215 average; he was traded to California the day after the season for a minor-league player.

Hayes missed six weeks with elbow surgery and Bedrosian was out the first two weeks with pneumonia, and Bradley, Samuel, and James all had below-par years. The club's .240 average and 4.14 ERA were the league's worst. Only Gross (12–14) and Carman (10–14) won in double figures.

239

First baseman Ricky Jordan, who joined the Phillies in 1988.

Outside of its won–lost record (67–95), the 1989 club barely resembled the previous year's edition. Ricky Jordan was at first base from the beginning; at second was Tommy Herr, who had used free agency to get to the Phillies; at short was Dickie Thon, obtained from San Diego; at third was Charlie Hayes, acquired from the Giants with pitchers Dennis Cook and Terry Mulholland in exchange for Bedrosian; in the outfield were John Kruk, over from San Diego for Chris James; and Lenny Dykstra, in from the Mets along with reliever Roger McDowell in a steal of a deal that saw Samuel go to New York. Other new recruits were right-hander Ken Howell, whom the Phillies got from Baltimore for Phil Bradley, and reliever Jeff Parrett, acquired from Montreal for Kevin Gross.

Charlie Hayes was at third base because Mike Schmidt had elected to retire rather than struggle

The sad state of affairs in 1988 gave opportunities to a couple of youngsters brought up from Maine, first baseman Ricky Jordan and outfielder Ron Jones. In sixty-nine games Jordan batted .308 and drove in 43 runs, while in thirty-three games Jones batted .290 with 26 RBIs.

Things didn't get better in 1989, not even with a spirited new skipper, Nick Leyva, recruited from the St. Louis Cardinal coaching staff. Leyva had been a minor-league infielder of little distinction and then, beginning at the age of twenty-four, a minor-league manager. Now, at the age of thirty-six, he had been handed the challenging task of trying to get the Phillies engine purring again. Nick, however, ended up in the same dark region as his predecessor, last place.

Nick Leyva, who took over as Phillies skipper in 1989.

Shortstop Dickie Thon, acquired from San Diego in 1989.

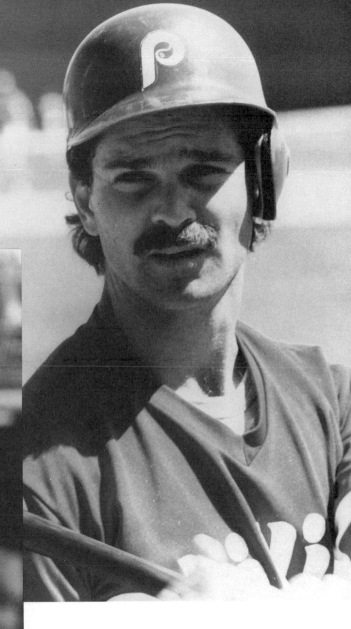

241

Tommy Herr, the veteran second baseman, was with the Phillies in 1989 and 1990.

Terry Mulholland acknowledging
the cheers of the crowd after
pitching a no-hitter against
the Giants at Veterans Stadium
on August 15, 1990.

John Kruk, outfielder–first baseman, whom the
Phillies got from San Diego in 1989.

Lenny Dykstra batted .325 in 1990.

Ken Howell joined the Phillies staff in 1989.

Reliever Roger McDowell.

244 on a ball field. On May 29, after 42 games, six home runs, and a .203 batting average, Schmidt gracefully accepted the cold reality that things were not going to get better. The Phillies were in San Francisco at the time, and referring to a couple of Giants stars, an emotionally overwrought Schmidt said, "I look at fellows like Will Clark and Kevin Mitchell and I see the player I used to be. It hurts to know that I'm no longer that player."

Voluntarily relinquishing the rest of the money on his lucrative contract rather than embarrass himself on a ball field, the player who many feel is the greatest in Phillies history, called it a career. Mike Schmidt's scroll of achievements include 548 home runs, 8 home run titles, 3 MVP awards, a pile of Gold Glove awards, just about every meaningful career offensive record in Phillies annals, and, in the words of one writer, "proof that you can be a superstar as well as an admirable human being."

Some of the trades engineered by new GM Lee

Catcher Darren Daulton, a Phillie since 1983.

Third baseman Charlie Hayes.

Thomas began paying dividends in 1989, while others would later. After having batted just .184 for San Diego earlier in the season, Kruk fired away at a .331 average in 81 games for the Phillies. Herr was a .287 hitter and made only 7 errors in 144 games at second base, and Thon batted .271 with 15 home runs.

With Schmidt gone, Von Hayes became the club's primary long-ball threat and responded with a career-high 26 crowd pleasers. Jordan gave the team a satisfactory .285 season, but Ron Jones, the other highly regarded young player from 1988, was lost for the season on April 18 after injuring his knee in a collision with the right field fence at Shea Stadium.

The club's best won–lost record in 1989 belonged to a reliever—Jeff Parrett, who was 12–6. Howell (12–12) was the only other man on the staff to win in double figures, with no other starter winning more than 6. With Bedrosian's departure, the closer's role devolved on sinker-balling right-hander Roger McDowell, a blithe spirit with a penchant for practical jokes (hot foots were a specialty). But Roger could pitch and did so handsomely for the Phillies, notching 19 saves and logging a 1.11 ERA for 57 innings of work.

The Phillies moved into the 1990s on a current of modest progress as Leyva moved the boys up to a fourth-place tie with the Cubs, their 77–85 record a 10-game improvement on 1989.

Much of the excitement for Phillies fans in the first half of the 1990 season was generated by Lenny Dykstra, whose hitting suddenly soared into the torrid zone. The man who had batted .237 the year before was batting .411 on May 25, climbed to .418 on June 4 and as late as June 8 was at .410, at which point gravity began taking over. Lenny's high-altitude hitting included a 23-game hitting streak, 3 games less than Chuck Klein's club record.

The single most scintillating performance by a Phillies player in the 1990 season was delivered on August 15 by left-hander Terry Mulholland. On that night Mulholland fired a 6–0 no-hitter against his former club, the San Francisco Giants. Only a seventh-inning throwing error by third baseman Charlie Hayes prevented Mulholland from having a perfect game, but Charlie atoned when with two out in the ninth he made a fine backhanded grab of pinch hitter Gary Carter's low line drive to end the game. Mulholland's was the first no-hitter by a Phillies pitcher since Rick Wise's in 1971 and the first pitched at home by a Phillies pitcher in the twentieth century.

The game of the year for the Phillies came six days later, on August 21, in Los Angeles. Trailing 11–1 after seven innings, they scored two runs in the eighth and then a stunning nine in the top of the ninth and held on for a 12–11 victory. After the game all that an incredulous Dodger manager Tommy Lasorda could say was, "I'm shocked. I don't believe it. I don't believe it." Well, as Ripley said . . .

On August 3 the Phillies made a surprise trade, acquiring thirty-four-year-old, two-time MVP out-

Von Hayes.

Dale Murphy. The veteran slugger joined the Phillies in August 1990.

and finished with an 8–7 record. Lefty Pat Combs was the top winner (10–10), followed by Mulholland (9–10). Darrell Akerfelds, Joe Boever, Don Carman, and Roger McDowell ran the bullpen, with McDowell recording 22 saves.

So the Phillies began the century's final decade on a note of improvement, a healthy sign in a game that thrives on hope and optimism, qualities that Phillies fans have often needed and never been short of. From Baker Bowl to Shibe Park to Veteran's Stadium, the memories have accumu-

Pat Combs, who broke in with four straight wins at the end of the 1989 season.

fielder Dale Murphy from the Braves in exchange for Jeff Parrett. It was the kind of trade usually made by contenders, sending off a younger player for an older one they hope can push them over the top. It was also strange in that Murphy's statistics had been in steady decline the past few years. Nevertheless, the Phillies believed he could still hit and that he would help.

At season's end Dykstra had long since descended from the nose-bleed heights of .400 and wound up with a .325 average, fourth best in the league and 57 points above his lifetime mark. With 192 hits, he tied for the league lead. Kruk batted .291, while Von Hayes led the squad with 17 homers and 73 RBIs.

The starting pitching was hurt when Ken Howell went down with midseason shoulder miseries

Veteran's Stadium.

lated, grown old, passed into history, but because in baseball past and present are inextricably one, those memories are never completely gone.

The high points of Phillies history are few and often far between—the pennants of 1915, 1950, 1980, and 1983, and above all the world championship of 1980—and because of this the memories are treasured and carefully nurtured. The pride of Philadelphia Phillies history rests with those pennants and the exploits of Sliding Billy Hamilton and Ed Delahanty, of Grover Cleveland Alexander and Chuck Klein, of Robin Roberts and Richie Ashburn, of Mike Schmidt and Steve Carlton, all of whom, along with their colleagues, have contributed wondrous moments to a city already rich with them.

HOME RUNS

1913	Cravath	19
1914	Cravath	19
1915	Cravath	24
1917	Cravath	12
1918	Cravath	8
1919	Cravath	12
1920	Williams	15
1923	Williams	41
1927	Williams	30
1929	Klein	43
1931	Klein	31
1932	Klein	38
1933	Klein	28
1974	Schmidt	36
1975	Schmidt	38
1976	Schmidt	38
1980	Schmidt	48
1981	Schmidt	31
1983	Schmidt	40
1984	Schmidt	36
1986	Schmidt	37

TRIPLES

1947	Walker	16
1950	Ashburn	14
1958	Ashburn	13
1962	Callison	10
1964	Allen	13
1965	Callison	16
1972	Bowa	13
1976	Cash	12
1984	Samuel	19
1987	Samuel	15

DOUBLES

1914	Magee	39
1916	Niehoff	42
1930	Klein	59
1933	Klein	44
1934	Allen	42
1966	Callison	40
1972	Montanez	39

HITS

1913	Cravath	179
1914	Magee	171
1929	O'Doul	254
1932	Klein	226
1933	Klein	223
1951	Ashburn	221
1953	Ashburn	205
1958	Ashburn	215
1975	Cash	213
1981	Rose	140
1990	Dykstra	192

RUNS BATTED IN

1900	Flick	110
1910	Magee	116
1913	Cravath	118
1914	Magee	101
1915	Cravath	118
1931	Klein	121
1932	Hurst	143
1933	Klein	120
1950	Ennis	126
1975	Luzinski	120
1980	Schmidt	121
1981	Schmidt	91
1984	Schmidt	106
1986	Schmidt	119

250

BATTING

1910	Magee	.331
1929	O'Doul	.398
1933	Klein	.368
1947	Walker	.363
1955	Ashburn	.338
1958	Ashburn	.350

WINS

1911	Alexander	28
1913	Seaton	27
1914	Alexander	27
1915	Alexander	31
1916	Alexander	33
1917	Alexander	30
1931	Elliott	19
1952	Roberts	28
1953	Roberts	23
1954	Roberts	23
1972	Carlton	27
1977	Carlton	23
1980	Carlton	24
1982	Carlton	23
1983	Denny	19

STRIKEOUTS

1912	Alexander	195
1913	Seaton	168
1914	Alexander	214
1915	Alexander	241
1916	Alexander	167
1917	Alexander	200
1940	Higbe	137
1953	Roberts	198
1954	Roberts	185
1957	Sanford	188
1967	Bunning	253
1972	Carlton	310
1974	Carlton	240
1980	Carlton	286
1982	Carlton	286
1983	Carlton	275

EARNED RUN AVERAGE

1915	Alexander	1.22
1916	Alexander	1.55
1917	Alexander	1.83
1972	Carlton	1.98

Abrams, Cal, *142*
Adams, Bert, 52, *59*
Adams, Elvin ("Buster"), 118, *120*
  statistics for, 1944, 122
Akerfields, Darrell, statistics for, 1990, 246
Alexander, Grover Cleveland, *45*, 45, *48*, *54*,
    58, 60, *61*, *89*, 247
  drafted, 61
  retirement, 89
  statistics for
    1910, 46
    1911, 46
    1912, 48
    1913, 51
    1915, 53
    1916, 53
  traded, 61
Allen, Ethan, *97*
  statistics for
    1934, 97
    1935, 100
Allen, Richie (Dick), 173, *174*, *180*, 185
  reacquired, 200
  Rookie of the Year, 1964, 178
  statistics for
    1964, 178
    1965, 179
    1966, 182
    1968, 184
Amaro, Ruben, *177*, *220*
American Association, 14, 21
American League, 31
Anderson, George ("Sparky"), *165*
  statistics for, 1959, 166
Anderson, Harry, 160, *161*
  statistics for, 1958, 165
Andrews, Ed, *18*
Anson, Adrian ("Cap"), 13
Arlett, Buzz, statistics for, 1931, 92
Arnovich, Morrie, *106*, *107*
  statistics for
    1938, 108
    1939, 108
Ashburn, Richie, 128, *129*, *140*, *151*, *157*,
    247
  statistics for
    1948, 131
    1950, 146
    1951, 146
    1952, 148
    1953, 149
    1954, 154
    1955, 155
    1956, 157
    1957, 160
    1958, 165
  traded, 166
Atwood, Bill, *103*

Baker Bowl, 49, 53, *76*, *95*
  final game, 103
  last game at, *104*
Baker, William F., 49, *65*

death of, 90
Baldschun, Jack, *170*, 170, 171, 178
  statistics for, 1962, 171
Bancroft, Dave, 52, *60*, *62*
  statistics for, 1915, 53
  traded, 66
Barrett, Dick, 117
  statistics for
    1943, 120
    1944, 122
    1945, 123
Barry, John ("Shad"), *32*
  statistics for, 1902, 31
Bartell, Dick, *90*, 90
  statistics for
    1932, 95
    1934, 97
  traded, 99
Baumgartner, Stan, *54*
Becker, Beals, *50*
  statistics for
    1913, 51
    1914, 51
Beck, Walter ("Boom-Boom"), *117*
Bedrosian, Steve, 233, 236, *238*, 239, 240
  Cy Young Award, 1987, 236
  statistics for, 1987, 236
Benge, Ray, *88*
  statistics for
    1928, 83
    1930, 85
    1931, 92
    1932, 95
Bennett, Dennis, *178*, 179
  statistics for, 1964, 178
Bentley, Jack, 76
Betts, Walter ("Huck"), *72*
Blaylock, Marv, *158*
Bochy, Bruce, *219*
Boever, Joe, statistics for, 1990, 246
Boone, Bob, 194, *208*
  statistics for
    1973, 194
    1977, 203
    1978, 210
Boozer, John, *176*
Borowy, Hank, *134*
  statistics for, 1949, 135
Bouchee, Ed, 160, *161*
  statistics for
    1958, 165
    1959, 166
Bowa, Larry, 191, *193*, *207*
  statistics for
    1970, 187
    1971, 189
    1975, 200
    1977, 203
    1978, 210
    1979, 213
Bowman, Joe, *102*
Boyle, "Honest Jack," statistics for, 1894, 25
Bradley, Phil, 239

Bragan, Bobby, *109*, *110*
  statistics for, 1940, 109
Bransfield, William ("Kitty"), *40*
  statistics for, 1908, 40
Brennan, Ad, *42*
  statistics for, 1913, 51
Brett, Ken, 194
  statistics for, 1973, 195
Briggs, Johnny, *181*
  statistics for, 1969, 185
Browne, Byron, 185
Brusstar, Warren, 207, *208*, 210
Buffinton, Charlie, *19*
  statistics for, 1887, 18
Buhl, Bob, 182
Bunning, Jim, *176*, 177, *179*, 186
  statistics for
    1964, 178
    1965, 179
    1966, 182
    1967, 183
    1970, 187
  traded, 183
Burgess, Forrest ("Smoky"), 146, *147*
  statistics for
    1952, 148
    1953, 149
    1954, 154
  traded, 155
Burns, Ed, *56*
Burns, George, 77
Buzhardt, John, *168*, 168, 171
Byrne, Bobby, *52*
Bystrom, Marty, *218*
  statistics for, 1980, 216

Callison, Johnny, *168*, 168, 170
  statistics for
    1962, 171
    1963, 171
    1964, 178
    1965, 179
    1969, 185
  traded, 186
Camilli, Dolph, 97, *98*
  statistics for
    1935, 100
    1936, 100
    1937, 100
  traded, 102
Campanella, Roy, *154*
Cardwell, Don, *166*
  statistics for, 1959, 166
Carlson, Hal, 73, *74*
  statistics for
    1925, 74
    1926, 76
Carlton, Steve, 189, *192*, *211*, *214*, *217*, 247
  Cy Young Award
    1972, 190
    1977, 207
    1980, 216
    1982, 226

Carlton, Steve (*continued*)
  statistics for
    1972, 190
    1973, 195
    1974, 198
    1975, 200
    1976, 202
    1977, 207
    1978, 210
    1979, 213
    1980, 216
    1981, 223
    1982, 226
    1983, 229
    1984, 231
    1986, 235
  traded, 235
Carman, Don, *235*, 246
  statistics for
    1986, 235
    1987, 239
    1988, 239
Carpenter, Robert R. M., owner, 120,
  131
Carpenter, Ruly, *195*
  president, 194
Casey, Dan, statistics for, 1887, 18
Cash, Dave, 196, *205*
  statistics for
    1974, 198
    1975, 200
Chalmers, George, *47*
Chapman, Ben, *131*
  manager, 124
Chiozza, Lou, *98*
  statistics for, 1934, 97
Christenson, Larry, *208*, 213
  statistics for
    1975, 200
    1976, 202
    1977, 207
    1978, 210
Church, Emory ("Bubba"), *138*
  statistics for, 1951, 146
Clark, Mel, *158*
Clay, Dain, 118
Clements, Jack, 17
Collins, Jimmy, 31
Collins, Phil, *87*
  statistics for
    1930, 85
    1931, 92
    1932, 95
Combs, Earle, *152*
Combs, Pat, *246*
  statistics for, 1990, 246
Conley, Gene, *164*, 166
  statistics for, 1959, 166
Connie Mack Stadium, *155*, *175*, 188
  under lights, *158*
  See also Baker Bowl
Cook, Dennis, 240
Cooke, Dusty, manager, 132
Coombs, "Colby Jack," 63
Corrales, Pat, *225*
  fired, 229
  manager, 224
  traded, 181
Corridon, Frank, *40*
Courtney, Ernie, *39*
Coveleski, Harry, 37, *38*
Covington, Wes, *172*
  statistics for, 1963, 171
Cox, William D.
  investigation of, 119–20
  owner, 116
Cravath, Clifford ("Gavvy"), *48*, 48, *55*, *57*, *64*
  statistics for
    1913, 49

1914, 51
1915, 53
1916, 59
1917, 60
1918, 62
  statistics as manager, 1919, 63
Crawford, Sam, 31
Cross, Lave, *22*, 22
  statistics for, 1894, 25
Cross, Monte, *32*
Culp, Ray, *172*
  statistics for, 1963, 171

Dahlgren, Babe, 117, *119*
  statistics for, 1943, 120
Dalrymple, Clay, *173*, 173
  statistics for, 1967, 183
"Dalton Gang," 166
Dark, Alvin, 168
Daulton, Darren, *244*
Davis, Curt, 97, *99*
  statistics for
    1932, 99
    1935, 100
Davis, Kiddo, statistics for, 1932, 95
Davis, Virgil ("Spud"), 78, *86*
  reacquired, 102
  statistics for
    1928, 83
    1930, 85
    1931, 92
    1932, 95
    1933, 96
  traded, 96
Dean, Wayland, 76
DeJesus, Ivan, *224*
  statistics for
    1981, 223
    1983, 228
Delahanty, Ed, *19*, 19, 20, 21, 22, *26*, 247
  death of, 32
  statistics for
    1892, 23
    1893, 23
    1894, 25
    1895, 25
    1896, 26
    1898, 27
    1899, 30
    1900, 31
    1901, 32
    1902, 32
Demaree, Al, 52, *54*, *58*
  statistics for
    1915, 53
    1916, 53
Demeter, Don, 170, *171*
  statistics for
    1962, 171
    1963, 173
  traded, 177
Denny, John, *229*, 231
  Cy Young Award, 1983, 229
  statistics for, 1983, 229
Diaz, Beaudilio ("Bo"), *228*, 231
  statistics for
    1982, 226
    1983, 228
Dickson, Murry, *153*
  statistics for, 1954, 154
Dillhoefer, Pickles, 61
DiMaggio, Dominic, *123*
DiMaggio, Joe, *123*
DiMaggio, Vince, *123*
  statistics for, 1945, 123
Donahue, Frank ("Red"), *29*, 32
  statistics for, 1899, 30
Donnelly, Sylvester ("Blix"), *132*
Donovan, Bill, 66

Dooin, Charles ("Red"), 34, *36*, 42
Doolan, Mickey, *37*, 37
Doyle, Denny, *189*
Drews, Karl, *150*, *153*
  statistic for, 1952, 148
"Dr. Strangeglove," 179
Dudley, Clise, 90
Duffy, Hugh, 33, *34*
Duggleby, Bill, *39*
Durham, Israel, 40
Dykstra, Lenny, 240, *242*, 245
  statistics for, 1990, 246

Early Pennants, 15
Eastern Division title winners, *203*
Eastwick, Rawley, 209
Elia, Lee, *237*
  manager, 236
Elliott, Hal, *88*
  statistics for, 1930, 86
Elliott, Jim ("Jumbo"), 90, *93*
  statistics for
    1931, 92
    1932, 95
Ennis, Del, *126*, *135*, *139*, *160*
  statistics for
    1945, 125
    1947, 128
    1948, 132
    1949, 135
    1950, 146
    1951, 146
    1952, 148
    1953, 149
    1954, 154
    1955, 155
    1956, 157
  traded, 157
Espinosa, Nino, statistics for, 1979, 213
Etten, Nick, *113*
  statistics for, 1941, 110
Ewing, Bob, *44*

Farrell, Dick, 160, *162*, 166
  reacquired, 183
  statistics for
    1957, 160
    1960, 168
    1967, 183
Fastest game, the, 64
Federal League, 51
Felske, John, *237*
  fired, 236
  manager, 232
Ferguson, Charlie, 15, *16*
  statistics for
    1886, 16
    1887, 18
Fernandez, Humberto ("Chico"), 160, *161*
First infielder to wear glove, 18
First night game, 99
First Pennant, 53
First year of divisional play, 184
Fitzsimmons, Freddie, *120*
  manager, 119
Fletcher, Art, 66, *67*, 72
Flick, Elmer, *28*
  statistics for
    1898, 27
    1899, 30
    1900, 31
    1901, 31
Flood, Curt, 185
Fogarty, Jim, 16, *17*, 22
Fogel, Horace, 42
Fonseca, Lew, 77
  statistics for, 1925, 74
Fox, Howie, 146
Foxx, Jimmie, *94*, *124*

statistics for, 1945, 123
Fraser, Chick, *33*
  no hitter, 1903, 33
  statistics for, 1899, 30
Freese, Gene, *164*
  statistics for, 1959, 166
Friberg, Barney, *80*
  statistics for, 1930, 85
Frick, Ford, *122*
Fryman, Woody, 183, *185*
  statistics for, 1968, 184
Fullis, Chuck, 96
  statistics for, 1933, 96

Gamble, Oscar, 186, *190*
Garber, Gene, *199*, 202, 207
  statistics for, 1975, 200
Geier, Phil, 26
Gerheauser, Al, *121*
  statistics for, 1943, 120
Giles, Bill, 224, *225*
Giles, Warren, *122*
Gleason, William ("Kid"), 18, *35*
  manager, 19
Glossop, Albie, *116*
Golden Age, 60
Goliat, Mike, *140*
Gonzalez, Tony, 168, 170, *183*
  statistics for
    1962, 171
    1963, 171
    1967, 182
    1968, 184
Gorbous, Glen, 155
Grace, Earl, 100, *101*
Grant, Eddie, 42, *43*
Green, Dallas, *169*, *215*, *221*
  manager, 214
  statistics for, 1960, 168
Greengrass, Jim, 155
Groat, Dick, 181
Gross, Greg, *223*
Gross, Kevin, *232*, 240
  statistics for
    1985, 233
    1986, 235
    1987, 239
    1988, 239

Haddix, Harvey, 157, *159*
Hall, Dick, *184*
  statistics for, 1967, 183
Hallman, Billy, *24*, 24
Hamey, Roy, general manager, 151
Hamilton, Billy, *21*, 21, 26, *247*
  statistics for
    1889, 22
    1891, 22
    1892, 23
    1893, 23
    1894, 25
    1895, 25
Hamner, Granny, 124, 128, *133*, *148*,
  149
  statistics for
    1950, 146
    1952, 148
  traded, 165
Hansen, Snipe, statistics for, 1932, 95
Harmon, Terry, *189*
Harper, George, 74, *77*
  statistics for
    1924, 73
    1925, 74
Harrell, Ray, *107*, 108
Harris, Bucky
  fired, 118
  manager, 117
Hawks, Louis ("Chicken"), statistics for,

1925, 74
Hayes, Charlie, 240, *244*
Hayes, Von, 226, *228*, 239, *245*
  statistics for
    1983, 228
    1984, 231
    1986, 233–35
    1989, 244
    1990, 246
Hearn, Jim, *162*
Hebner, Richie, 203, *206*
  statistics for
    1977, 203
    1978, 210
  traded, 213
Heintzelman, Ken, *134*
  statistics for, 1949, 135
Hemsley, Rollie, *127*
Hemus, Solly, *163*
  statistics for, 1958, 165
Henline, Walter ("Butch"), 69, *70*
  statistics for, 1923, 72
Hernandez, Willie, statistics for, 1983,
  229
Herrera, Pancho, 168
Herr, Tommy, 240, *241*
  statistics for, 1989, 244
Higbe, Kirby, *107*, 108, *111*
  statistics for, 1940, 109
Highest-scoring game box score, *71*
Highest-scoring game, the, 71
Hisle, Larry, *188*
  statistics for
    1969, 185
    1970, 187
Hoak, Don, 173, *174*
Hoerner, Joe, 185, *191*
Hoerst, Frank, *118*
Holke, Walter
  statistics for
    1923, 72
    1924, 73
Holland, Al, *227*
  statistics for, 1983, 229
Holley, Ed
  statistics for
    1932, 95
    1933, 96
Hollingsworth, Al, 102
Howell, Ken, 240, *243*
  statistics for
    1989, 244
    1990, 246
Hubbell, Bill, 66, *67*
  statistics for, 1924, 73
Hughes, Tommy, *114*
  statistics for
    1941, 111
    1942, 116
Hulbert, William, 13, *14*, 14, *15*
Hurst, Don, *81*, *93*
  statistics for
    1928, 80, 83
    1930, 85
    1931, 92
    1932, 95
  traded, 97
Hutton, Tom, 203, *206*

Irwin, Arthur, 18, 23

Jacklitsch, Fred, *37*
Jackson, Grant, *186*
  statistics for, 1969, 185
Jackson, Larry, *182*, 182
  statistics for
    1966, 182
    1967, 183
    1968, 184

James, Chris, 239
  statistics for, 1987, 239
Jenkins, Ferguson, 181
  traded, 182
Johnson, Alex, traded, 181
Johnson, Ban, 31
Johnson, Dave, 203
Johnson, Deron, *187*
  statistics for
    1968, 184
    1969, 185
    1970, 187
    1971, 188–89
Johnson, Jerry, traded, 185
Johnson, Silas, *112*
Johnson, Sylvester, *97*, 97
Johnstone, Jay, *199*
  statistics for
    1975, 200
    1976, 201
    1977, 203
Jones, Ron
  statistics for
    1988, 240
    1989, 244
Jones, Willie ("Puddin' Head"), 128, *139*,
  146, *156*, *159*
  statistics for
    1949, 135
    1950, 146
  traded, 165
Jordan, Ricky, *240*
  statistics for
    1988, 240
    1989, 244
Judd, Oscar, statistics for, 1946, 125–26

Kaat, Jim, 200, *204*
  statistics for, 1976, 202
Karl, Anton (Andy), *124*
  statistics for, 1945, 123
Kazanski, Ted, 151, *152*
Keefe, Tim, *24*, 24
Keeler, Willie, 31
Killefer, Bill, *49*, 49, 61
Kimmick, Wally, 77
Klein, Chuck, 79, *81*, *85*, *92*, *94*, *96*, *108*,
  247
  MVP, 1932, 95
  reacquired, 100
  statistics for
    1928, 80, 83
    1930, 85, 86
    1931, 92
    1933, 96
    1936, 100
    1937, 102
    1938, 108
  traded, 96
Klippstein, Johnny, 171, *172*
Knabe, Otto, *42*
Knowles, Darold, statistics for, 1966,
  182
Konetchy, Ed, 66
Konstanty, Jim, *138*, *145*, 145, 154
  MVP, 1950, 146
  statistics for
    1948, 132
    1949, 135
    1950, 146
    1951, 146
    1953, 149
Koosman, Jerry, *231*
  statistics for
    1984, 231
    1985, 233
Kruk, John, *242*
  statistics for
    1989, 244

Kruk, John (*continued*)
  1990, 246
  traded, 240
Krukow, Mike, statistics for, 1982, 226

Lajoie, Napoleon, 26, *27*
  statistics for
    1897, 27
    1898, 27
    1899, 30
    1900, 31
LaMaster, Wayne, *105*
  statistics for, 1937, 102
Landis, Kenesaw Mountain, 66, 119–20
Lavagetto, Cookie, *110*
Leach, Freddy, *77*
  statistics for
    1926, 76
    1927, 77
LeBourveau, DeWitt Wiley ("Bevo"), *69*, 69
Lee, Cliff, *71*
Lee, Hal, statistics for, 1932, 95
Leonard, Emil ("Dutch"), *129*
  statistics for
    1947, 128
    1948, 132
Lerch, Randy, *211*
  statistics for
    1977, 207
    1978, 210
Lerian, Walt, 83
Leyva, Nick, *240*
  manager, 240
Litwhiler, Danny, *111, 119*
  statistics for
    1940, 109
    1941, 110
    1942, 111
  traded, 118
Livingston, Thompson ("Mickey"), *115*
Lobert, Hans, *46*, 46, *115*
  manager, 111
  statistics for, 1913, 51
Locke, William H., 49
Lonborg, Jim, 194, *204*
  statistics for
    1973, 195
    1974, 198
    1975, 200
    1976, 202
    1977, 207
Lopata, Stan, *142, 159*
  statistics for
    1953, 149
    1954, 154
    1956, 157
  traded, 165
Lopat, Eddie, *145*
Lucchesi, Frank, *188*
  manager, 185
Luderus, Fred, 46, *47, 56, 60*
  statistics for
    1915, 53
    1916, 59
Lush, Johnny, no hitter, 1906, 37
Luzinski, Greg, *195, 207*
  statistics for
    1972, 194
    1973, 194
    1975, 200
    1976, 201
    1977, 203
    1978, 210
    1980, 216
Lyle, Albert ("Sparky"), *222*
Lynch, Tom, 49

McBride, Bake, 203, *206*
  statistics for

1977, 207
1980, 216
McCarver, Tim, 185, 187, *192, 214*
McCormick, Frank, *107, 125*
  statistics for, 1946, 125
McCurdy, Harry, *87*
  statistics for, 1930, 85
McDowell, Roger, 240, *243*, 246
  statistics for, 1989, 245
McFarland, Ed, 27
McGraw, John, 31, *79*
McGraw, Tug, 198, 202, *203*, 207, 210, *212*,
  216, *218, 220*
  statistics for, 1975, 200
McInnis, John ("Stuffy"), 76, *78*
Mack, Connie, 31
McLish, Cal, *170*
  statistics for
    1962, 171
    1963, 171
McNichol, James P., 40
McQuillan, George, 38, *39, 54*
  statistics for
    1908, 40
    1909, 40–42
Maddox, Garry, 198, *202*, 231
  statistics for
    1975, 200
    1976, 201
    1978, 210
    1980, 216
    1982, 226
    1983, 228
Madlock, Bill, *193*
Magee, Sherry, *35, 50*
  statistics for
    1904, 34
    1907, 38
    1910, 44
    1913, 51
    1914, 51
Mahaffey, Art, *169*
  statistics for
    1960, 168
    1961, 170
    1962, 171
    1963, 171
    1964, 178
  traded, 181
Mallon, Les, statistics for, 1931, 92
Marston, Charlie, 26
Martin, Herschel, *106*
  statistics for, 1938, 108
Martin, Jerry, *209*
Marty, Joe, *107*, 108
Matthews, Gary, *222*
  statistics for
    1981, 223
    1983, 228
Matuszek, Len, statistics for, 1984, 231
Mauch, Gene, *167*
  fired, 183
  manager, 167
Mayer, Erskine, *54, 56*
  statistics for
    1913, 51
    1915, 53
    1916, 53
    1917, 60
May, Merrill ("Pinky"), *109*
  statistics for
    1940, 109
    1943, 120
  in World War II, 121
Meadows, Lee, 66
  statistics for
    1919, 64
    1920, 65
    1921, 69

Melton, Rube, *117*
  statistics for, 1942, 116
Meusel, Emil ("Irish"), *63, 70*
  statistics for
    1918, 62
    1919, 63
    1920, 65
    1921, 69
Meyer, Jack, 157, *160*, 166
Meyer, Russ, *149*
  statistics for
    1949, 135
    1952, 148
Miller, Bob, *139, 156*
Miller, Eddie, *131, 133*
Miller, Roy ("Doc"), *50*
Miller, Russ
  statistics for
    1928, 83
    1950, 146
Miller, Stu, 157
Mills, A. G., 15
Mitchell, Clarence, *72*, 72, 77
  statistics for, 1925, 74
Mokan, Johnny
  statistics for
    1923, 72
    1925, 74
    1926, 76
Money, Don, 183, 191, *193*
  traded, 194
Montanez, Willie, 186, *198*
  statistics for
    1971, 189
    1974, 198
  traded, 198
Moore, Earl, *41*
  statistics for, 1909, 40
Moore, Johnny, *102*
  statistics for
    1934, 97
    1935, 100
    1936, 100
    1937, 102
Moore, Terry, *152*
  manager, 151
Moran, Pat, 52, *53*
Moren, Lew, *41*
  statistics for, 1909, 40
Morgan, Bobby, *154*, 157, 160
Morgan, Joe, *227*, 228
  statistics for, 1983, 228
Mulcahy, Hugh, *105*
  statistics for
    1937, 102
    1938, 108
    1940, 109
Mulholland, Terry, 240, *242*
  no hitter 1990, 245
  statistics for, 1990, 246
Mulvey, Joe, *17*
Murphy, Dale, *246*, 246
Murray, Bill, 37
Murtaugh, Danny, *113*
  statistics for, 1941, 110
  in World War II, 121
Myatt, George, manager, 185

Nash, Billy, 26
National Association, 13
National League, 21
  early years, 14
  expansion, 1962, 170
  expansion, 1969, 184
  playoffs
    1976, 202
    1977, 209
    1978, 210–11
    1980, 216–17

1981, 223
1983, 229–30
Neeman, Cal, 168
Newsome, Lamar ("Skeeter"), *126*
  statistics for, 1946, 125
Nicholson, Bill, 132, *148*
Niehoff, Bert, 52, *60, 62*
Northey, Ron, *116,* 125, *126*
  statistics for
    1942, 116
    1943, 120
    1944, 122
Nugent, Gerry, *115*
Nugent, May Mallon, 90

O'Doul, Frank ("Lefty"), *83, 86*
  statistics for
    1929, 83
    1930, 85
Oeschger, Joe, 54, *61*
  statistics for, 1917, 60
O'Neill, Steve, *152*
  fired, 151
  manager, 148
Orth, Al, *29,* 32
Owens, Jim, *166*
  statistics for, 1959, 166
Owens, Paul, *229*
  general manager, 194
Ozark, Danny, *201*
  fired, 213
  manager, 194

Parkinson, Frank, 66, *68*
Parrett, Jeff, 240
  statistics for, 1989, 244
Parrish, Lance, *236,* 236
  statistics for
    1987, 239
    1988, 239
Paskert, George ("Dode"), *46,* 46,
  57
  statistics for, 1916, 59
Passeau, Claude, 100, *101*
  statistics for
    1936, 100
    1937, 102
    1938, 108
  traded, 108
Paulette, Gene, 66
Pearce, Harry, *64*
Pearson, Isaac ("Ike"), *119*
Peel, Homer, 78
Pennant
  1950, 137–45, *144*
  1980, 219
Pennock, Herb, *122*
  death of, 131
  general manager, 121
Perez, Tony, 228
Philley, Dave, *164*
  statistics for, 1958, 165
Phillies league leaders, 249–50
Piatt, Wiley
  statistics for
    1898, 27
    1899, 30
Pittinger, Charles ("Togie"), *36*
  statistics for, 1905, 37
Players' League, 1890, 14
Players' League, 21
  collapse, 22
Podgajny, Johnny, *114*
  statistics for, 1941, 111
Post, Wally, *165*
  statistics for, 1959, 166
Potter, James, 33
Power, Vic, 178
Prendergast, Mike, 61

Prendergast, Mike, 61
Prothro, James ("Doc"), *107*
  manager, 108

Quinn, John, general manager, 165, 185

Raffensberger, Ken, *123*
  statistics for, 1944, 122
Rawley, Shane, *238*
  statistics for
    1984, 231
    1985, 233
    1987, 239
Reach, Alfred J., 13, 15, 18, 19, 21, 26
  leaving baseball, 33
Record, attendance
  1916, 125
  1946, 125
Reed, Ron, 200, 202, 207, 210, *212,* 216,
  220
  statistics for, 1983, 229
Repulski, Rip, 157
Rhem, Flint, statistics for, 1932, 95
Ridzik, Steve, *157*
Ring, Jimmy, *69,* 69, 72, 77
  statistics for
    1921, 69
    1924, 73
    1925, 74
    1926, 83
  traded, 74
Rixey, Eppa, *59*
  drafted, 63
  statistics for
    1912, 48
    1913, 51
    1915, 53
    1916, 53
    1917, 60
    1919, 64
    1920, 65
Rizzo, Johnny, statistics for, 1940, 109
Roberts, Robin, *130, 137, 149,* 149, *153, 155,*
  156, 163, 247
  signed, 129
  sold, 170
  statistics for
    1948, 132
    1949, 135
    1950, 146
    1951, 146
    1952, 148
    1954, 154
    1955, 155
    1956, 157
    1957, 160
    1958, 165
    1959, 166
    1960, 168
Robinson, Bill, *194*
  statistics for, 1973, 194
Roebuck, Ed, 178, *180*
Rogers, John, 21, 22, 26
  leaving baseball, 33
Rogovin, Saul, 157
Rojas, Octavio ("Cookie"), *181*
  statistics for, 1965, 179
  traded, 185
Rose, Pete, *212, 213, 219, 221, 226,* 228
  statistics for
    1979, 213
    1980, 216
    1981, 223
Rowe, Lynwood ("Schoolboy"), 117, *121*
  statistics for
    1943, 120
    1946, 125
    1947, 128
    1948, 132

in World War II, 121
Ruffin, Bruce, *236*
  statistics for
    1986, 235
    1987, 239
Ruth, Babe, final major-league game, 100
Ruthven, Dick, 209, *210,* 213
  statistics for
    1978, 210
    1980, 216
    1981, 223
    1982, 226
Ryan, Connie, 146, *147*
Ryan, Mike, 187, *190*
  statistics for, 1969, 185

Samuel, Juan, *231,* 239
  statistics for
    1984, 230–31
    1985, 233
    1987, 239
Sandberg, Ryne, *224*
  statistics for, 1981, 223
Sanders, Ken, 194
Sand, John ("Heinie"), *80*
Sanford, Jack, 160, *162*
  Rookie of the Year, 1957, 160
  statistics for
    1957, 160
    1958, 165
  traded, 165
Sawyer, Eddie, *138*
  fired, 148
  manager, 132
  manager again, 163
  resignation, 167
Schanz, Charley, *122*
  statistics for, 1944, 122
Scharein, George, *106*
Schmidt, Mike, 194, 195, *197, 202, 203, 213,*
  213, 216, 230, 235, 239, 247
  MVP
    1980, 216
    1981, 223
    1986, 233
  retirement of, 240–44
  statistics for
    1973, 196
    1974, 196
    1975, 200
    1976, 201
    1977, 203
    1978, 210
    1980, 216
    1981, 223
    1982, 226
    1984, 230
    1986, 233
    1987, 239
    1988, 239
Schueler, Ron, *198*
  statistics for, 1974, 198
Schu, Rick, *233*
  statistics for, 1985, 233
Seaton, Tom, *51*
  statistics for
    1912, 48
    1913, 51
Selma, Dick, 186
Seminick, Andy, 118, 124, *127, 128, 141,*
  155
  statistics for
    1949, 135
    1950, 146
Semproch, Ray, *164*
  statistics for, 1958, 165
Sherlock, Monk, statistics for, 1930, 85
Shettsline, Bill, 27
Shibe, Ben, 15, 31

256

Shibe Park, *104, 112, 118*
  move to, 103
Short, Chris, *169, 180, 182*
  statistics for
    1960, 168
    1962, 171
    1963, 171
    1964, 178
    1965, 179
    1966, 182
    1967, 183
    1968, 184
    1970, 187
Shotton, Burt, 78, 79
Sievers, Roy, *171*
  statistics for
    1962, 171
    1963, 173
Simmons, Curt, 128, *130, 141, 150, 153*
  statistics for
    1948, 132
    1950, 146
    1952, 148
    1953, 149
    1954, 154
    1958, 165
Sisler, Dick, 131, *142, 143, 144,* 146
  statistics for, 1950, 146
Sizemore, Ted, 203
  statistics for, 1977, 203
Skinner, Bob
  manager, 183
  resignation, 185
Slagle, Jimmy, statistics for, 1900, 31
Smith, Charley, 171
Smith, George, *67*
  statistics for
    1920, 65
    1921, 69
Smith, Lonnie, *217*
  statistics for, 1980, 216
Smith, Mayo, *156*
  fired, 163
  manager, 154
Snider, Duke, *141*
Sparks, Tully, statistics for, 1906, 37
Speaker, Tris, *55*
Stallings, George, 27
Steinhagen, Ruth Ann, 136
Stengel, Charles Dillon ("Casey"), *66*
  statistics for, 1920, 65
Stephenson, Earl, 194
Stewart, Dave, 236
Stock, Milt, 52, *58, 60*
  statistics for, 1916, 59
Stuart, Dick, statistics for, 1965, 179
Sweetland, Les, *82*
  statistics for
    1928, 83
    1930, 85

Tabor, Jim, *126*
  statistics for, 1946, 125
Taylor, Tony, *167,* 168, 170
  statistics for
    1960, 168
    1963, 173
Tekulve, Kent, *232,* 236, 239
  statistics for, 1985, 233
Terry, Bill, *92*
Thomas, Frank, *180*
  statistics for, 1964, 178
Thomas, Lee, general manager, 244
Thomas, Roy, *34*
  statistics for
    1899, 30

    1904, 34
Thompson, Fresco, *78*
  statistics for
    1927, 77
    1928, 83
Thompson, Milt, 233, *234*
  statistics for, 1987, 239
Thompson, Sam, *20,* 21, *25*
  statistics for
    1887, 20
    1888, 20
    1892, 23
    1893, 23
    1894, 25
    1895, 25
    1896, 26
Thon, Dickie, 240, *241*
  statistics for, 1989, 244
Tierney, Cotton, statistics for, 1923, 72
Tincup, Ben, *54*
Titus, "Silent John," *35*
  statistics for, 1904, 34
Todd, Al, *98*
  statistics for, 1934, 97
Torgeson, Earl, *153, 154,* 154
Triandos, Gus, *177,* 177
Trillo, Manny, 213, *217*
  statistics for, 1980, 216
Triplett, Coaker, 118
Turner, Tuck, statistics for, 1894, 25
Twitchell, Wayne, *196*
  statistics for, 1973, 195

Uecker, Bob, 181
Underwood, Tom, *205*
  statistics for
    1975, 200
    1976, 202
Union Association (1884), 14
Unser, Del, *196*
  statistics for, 1973, 194

Verban, Emil, *126*
  statistics for
    1946, 125
    1947, 128
Veteran's Stadium, 188, *247*
Virgil, Ozzie, *234*
  statistics for, 1985, 233

Waitkus, Eddie, *135, 145*
  near murder, 135
  statistics for
    1950, 146
    1952, 148
Walk, Bob, *218*
  statistics for, 1980, 216
Walker, Curt, 69, *70*
Walker, Harry ("The Hat"), *128*
  statistics for
    1947, 128
    1948, 132
Walls, Lee, 168
Walters, Bucky, *99,* 99
  statistics for
    1935, 100
    1936, 100
    1937, 102
  traded, 102
Warren, Bennie, *114*
Wasdell, Jimmy, 117
Wehmeier, Herman, statistics for, 1954, 154
Weintraub, Phil, statistics for, 1938, 108
Western League, 30, 31
Weyhing, Gus, 22, *23*
  statistics for, 1892, 23

"Wheeze Kids," 228
White, Bill, 181, *183*
  statistics for, 1966, 182
Whitney, Arthur ("Pinky"), *90*
  statistics for
    1928, 80, 83
    1930, 85
    1932, 95
    1936, 100
    1937, 100
Whitted, George ("Possum"), 52, *57*
  statistics for
    1915, 53
    1916, 59
"Whiz Kids," 137
Wilhelm, Irvin ("Kaiser"), 66, *68*
Williams, Cy, 62, *63, 73, 75*
  statistics for
    1918, 62
    1920, 65
    1921, 69
    1923, 72
    1925, 74
    1926, 76
    1927, 77
Willoughby, Claude, *82*
  statistics for
    1928, 83
    1929, 84
    1930, 86
Wilson, Glenn, 231, *233*
  statistics for
    1985, 233
    1987, 239
Wilson, Jimmie, *73,* 73, *100*
  as manager, 96
  resignation, 108
  statistics for
    1925, 74
    1926, 76
Wine, Bobby, *173,* 173
  statistics for, 1967, 182–83
Winters, Jesse, 69
Wise, Rick, 178, *184, 191*
  statistics for
    1967, 183
    1969, 185
    1970, 187
    1971, 188
  traded, 189
Wolf, Clarence, 40
World Series
  1915, 53
  1950, 145–46
  1980, 219–21
  1983, 230
World War I, effect, 59, 63
World War II
  effect, 110
  end, 122
Wright, Harry, 15, *16,* 19, 20, 23
Wrightstone, Russ, 66, *68*
  statistics for
    1924, 73
    1925, 74
    1926, 76
    1927, 77
Wyrostek, Johnny, 125, *127*
  statistics for, 1952, 148

"Year of the Pitcher," 1968, 184
Young, Cy, 31
Young, Del, *105*

Zimmer, Charles ("Chief"), 33